Digital Access and Museums as Platforms

Digital Access and Museums as Platforms draws on interviews with museum practitioners, along with a range of case studies from public and private institutions, in order to investigate the tensions and benefits involved in making cultural collections available using digital technologies.

Taking a media and critical studies approach to the museum and raising questions about the role of privately owned search engines in facilitating museum experiences, the book questions who collects what, for whom objects are collected and what purpose these objects and collections serve. Connecting fieldwork undertaken in Australia and New Zealand with the global practices of technology companies, Wilson-Barnao brings attention to an emerging new model of digital ownership and moderation. Considering the synergising of these institutions with media systems, which are now playing a more prominent role in facilitating access to culture, the book also explores the motivations of different cultural workers for constructing the museum as a mediatised location.

Digital Access and Museums as Platforms will be of interest to academics and students working in the fields of museum studies, art, culture, media studies and digital humanities. Weighing in on conversations about how technologies are being incorporated into museums, the book should also be useful to practitioners working in museums and galleries around the world.

Caroline Wilson-Barnao is a lecturer in the School of Communication and Arts at the University of Queensland and completed her PhD in 2017. Her career spans two decades of experience in communication and marketing, supporting non-profit, arts organisations and in the corporate sector. She currently teaches in theory and practical subjects. Her research takes a critical focus on the use of digital media in museums, and in 2019 she filled the position of acting director of the master of museum studies programme at the University of Queensland.

Museums in Focus
Series Editor: Kylie Message, Australian National University, Australia

Committed to the articulation of big, even risky ideas, in small format publications, 'Museums in Focus' challenges authors and readers to experiment with, innovate, and press museums and the intellectual frameworks through which we view these. It offers a platform for approaches that radically rethink the relationships between cultural and intellectual dissent and crisis and debates about museums, politics and the broader public sphere.

'Museums in Focus' is motivated by the intellectual hypothesis that museums are not innately 'useful', 'safe' or even 'public' places, and that recalibrating our thinking about them might benefit from adopting a more radical and oppositional form of logic and approach. Examining this problem requires a level of comfort with (or at least tolerance of) the idea of crisis, dissent, protest and radical thinking, and authors might benefit from considering how cultural and intellectual crisis, regeneration and anxiety have been dealt with in other disciplines and contexts.

The following list includes only the most-recent titles to publish within the series. A list of the full catalogue of titles is available at: www.routledge.com/Museums-in-Focus/book-series/MIF

Museums and Atlantic Slavery
Ana Lucia Araujo

Digital Access and Museums as Platforms
Caroline Wilson-Barnao

https://www.routledge.com/Museums-in-Focus/book-series/MIF

MUSEUMS IN FOCUS

Logo by James Verdon (2017)

Digital Access and Museums as Platforms

Caroline Wilson-Barnao

LONDON AND NEW YORK

First published 2022
by Routledge
2 Park Square, Milton Park, Abingdon, Oxon OX14 4RN

and by Routledge
605 Third Avenue, New York, NY 10158

Routledge is an imprint of the Taylor & Francis Group, an informa business

© 2022 Caroline Wilson-Barnao

The right of Caroline Wilson-Barnao to be identified as author of this work has been asserted by her in accordance with sections 77 and 78 of the Copyright, Designs and Patents Act 1988.

All rights reserved. No part of this book may be reprinted or reproduced or utilised in any form or by any electronic, mechanical, or other means, now known or hereafter invented, including photocopying and recording, or in any information storage or retrieval system, without permission in writing from the publishers.

Trademark notice: Product or corporate names may be trademarks or registered trademarks, and are used only for identification and explanation without intent to infringe.

British Library Cataloguing-in-Publication Data
A catalogue record for this book is available from the British Library

Library of Congress Cataloging-in-Publication Data
Names: Wilson-Barnao, Caroline, author.
Title: Digital access and museums as platforms / Caroline Wilson-Barnao.
Description: Abingdon, Oxon ; New York, NY : Routledge, 2022. | Series: Museums in focus | Includes bibliographical references and index.
Identifiers: LCCN 2021020582 (print) | LCCN 2021020583 (ebook) | ISBN 9780367279141 (hardback) | ISBN 9781032104676 (paperback) | ISBN 9780429298691 (ebook)
Subjects: LCSH: Museum techniques—Technological innovations—Australia. | Museum techniques—Technological innovations—New Zealand. | Museums and the Internet—Australia. | Museums and the Internet—New Zealand. | Museum information networks—Australia. | Museum information networks—New Zealand. | Virtual museums—Australia. | Virtual museums—New Zealand.
Classification: LCC AM7 .W555 2022 (print) | LCC AM7 (ebook) | DDC 069/.4093—dc23
LC record available at https://lccn.loc.gov/2021020582
LC ebook record available at https://lccn.loc.gov/2021020583

ISBN: 978-0-367-27914-1 (hbk)
ISBN: 978-1-032-10467-6 (pbk)
ISBN: 978-0-429-29869-1 (ebk)

DOI: 10.4324/9780429298691

Typeset in Times New Roman
by Apex CoVantage, LLC

Anonymous graffiti, Athens. Image and logo by James Verdon (2017).

Contents

List of figures viii
Acknowledgements x

1 Introduction: from the analogue to the digital museum 1

2 The logic of open access to culture 19

3 From sensory to sensing museum 38

4 From museum to platform 57

5 Negotiating museums as platforms 75

Index 93

Figures

1.1 Selfie stations are a common way for museums to encourage visitors to share their experiences with social media networks, where families playfully engage with exhibits by having their picture taken. 5
1.2 This illustration depicts an art exhibition that has been configured specifically for visitors to engage with using cameras and smartphones. 7
1.3 This picture shows the Google Arts and Culture face-matching app, where users load images of themselves on an app, which are then matched with portraits resembling them housed in international museum collections. 13
2.1 The museum works towards making itself available to multiple publics through the provision of welcoming spaces. This picture depicts pram parking outside a children's activity corner. 26
2.2 This image, titled *Portrait of an Articulated Skeleton on a Bentwood Chair* (c. 1900) is in the Powerhouse Museum collection on Flickr and was a gift of the estate of Raymond W. Phillips (2008). It has been viewed 1,072,037 times, with 4,292 favs and 588 comments with users playfully engaging with the image by tagging and commenting. 32
2.3 Museum visitor photographing 'Say cheese please, but they can't'. 33
3.1 James Turrell's Amarna at MONA, 2015. 41
3.2 The 'O' pod at MONA. 42
3.3 Signage at exhibitions encourages visitors to document and share their experiences on social media using hashtags and posting. This image depicts a sign at the APT9 exhibition at QGoMA, Brisbane, Australia. 49

Figures ix

4.1 Museum experiences are now both virtual and physical, where digital technologies can enrich the museum experience and provide a host of new opportunities for visitors to engage with collections. 61

4.2 Visitor smartphones and apps are an important resource, providing layers of additional content such as music and artist interviews to enhance the museum experience. 62

4.3 This diagram demonstrates the relationship between a GAC-type platform and the end user, showing the benefit to the institution of creating this relationship. 68

4.4 Users can take photographs of themselves using Art Transfer on the GAC app, which applies an art filter to create an output that places the user into iconic artworks. 69

5.1 This image, *Portrait of Edmond de Belamy*, by art collective Obvious, was generated by AI and was sold at auction by Christie's for $432,000. 79

5.2 This screenshot of Creative Commons example of *La Mona Lisa* by Jesus Belzunce is licensed under CC BY-NC-ND 2.0. 82

5.3 *The Real Mona Lisa* by Nathan Shipley. This artist uses AI to re-create what important historical figures such as Mona Lisa might look like. 87

Acknowledgements

This book would not have come to fruition without the ongoing support and guidance of my academic colleagues and friends, especially Dr Nicholas Carah, Dr Zala Volcic and the late Professor Tom O'Regan. Thanks also to the University of Queensland School of Communication and Arts for the provision of funds to complete interstate and overseas research and to Assistant Professor Robyn Lincoln and Emeritus Professor Paul Wilson for viewing endless revisions.

It is also important to acknowledge the cultural professionals who agreed to make their spaces available and participate in interviews and who provided reference materials. The names and titles of the interviewees have been hidden to protect their professional identities.

To my family, special thanks are due to my husband Andrew, my mother Elizabeth and my children Olive and Hunter, who accompanied me on visits to different institutions.

Finally, I want to thank Kylie Message, Heidi Lowther, Kangan Gupta and Manas Roy at Routledge for their conceptual and editorial wisdom and Susan Jarvis for her significant contribution to this book.

1 Introduction

From the analogue to the digital museum

Introduction: platformisation of the museum

This book considers how museums have been radically reimagined by digital devices, social media platforms and ubiquitous networked communication enfolded into everyday life. The museum is increasingly operating in the context of the 'sharing economy' and 'participatory culture', where platforms and devices facilitate new forms of sociality (Bruns 2008; Jenkins, Ford and Green 2013). By acknowledging the inherent differences between the core missions of the art gallery, library, archive and museum, this book is concerned with their evolving role and their transition from essentially government or private institutions towards infrastructures of 'civil society' with new accountabilities (Blakenberg and Lord 2015: 22). The book argues for the adoption of a critical lens through which to regard this shift to the new media economy and puts forward a framework for examining these changes in the following chapters. However, the focus is not only on new technologies but also on the place of the museum in the public sphere. These once-authoritative formulators of predominantly heritage culture have been enlarging their practices beyond the exhibitory, educative and participatory to embrace making their space more social and inclusive.

At first glance, museums and their allied iterations as galleries, libraries and archives continue to curate exhibitions to educate and entertain their on-site visitors. Physical museums still perform that important civic function, and viewing an exhibition in the twenty-first century remains an experience involving artefacts housed in 'cabinets of curiosity' as they were in the 1600s, but now more publicly visible (Bennett 1998: 346). Pressure to democratise from the middle of the past century led cultural institutions to realise the need to engage with their audiences if they were to retain currency and remain financially viable (Witcomb 2003). These transformations have accelerated as the museum has increasingly embraced digital media technologies to permit visitors with smartphone in hand to experience its

DOI: 10.4324/9780429298691-1

cultural offerings, bringing about an interactive and participatory turn (Henning 2017). The trajectory of change is ongoing as global audiences can now readily access and freely interact with high-resolution images of collections that are made available in the online domain.

In this sense, museum collections are no longer housed exclusively within institutional walls nor are they only sites where visitors engage with each other and objects. Contemporary users, accustomed to social and streamed media sites where they connect, comment and rate, have prompted cultural institutions to rethink how they go about harnessing the digital to engage visitors and project relevance. High-speed internet, virtual reality (VR), three-dimensional (3D) scans and artificial intelligence (AI) make personalised visits possible, enabling audiences to access some of the world's greatest collections remotely, while on-site visitors use apps and interactive guides, post photographs to a range of media platforms and employ search engines for additional content about exhibits (Wilson-Barnao 2016, 2017, 2018, 2020). User data are then aggregated to feed into algorithms, which create the potential for museums to measure the impacts of culture and afford new means by which to make sense of collections.

Regardless of their funding sources, museums rightly possess a public ethos that is potentially altered by the entanglement of cultural offerings with the digital economy, and this ethos is a primary focus of this book. The museum has long been depicted as in service to society that 'acquires, conserves, researches, communicates, and exhibits the tangible and intangible heritage of humanity and its environment for the purposes of education, study, and enjoyment' (ICOM 2019: Statutes, Article 3, Section 1). Having drawn upon this characterisation for almost 50 years, the peak body the International Council of Museums (ICOM) sparked international debate when it recently put forward an alternate definition that eschewed a colonial context. The revised designation incorporates a remit to uphold 'social justice, global equality and planetary wellbeing' in addition to working 'in active partnership with and for diverse communities to collect, preserve, research, interpret, exhibit, and enhance understandings of the world' (ICOM 2019). The museum, as it is envisaged by ICOM, is not defined solely by the artefacts held within its virtual or physical spaces; rather, it is obliged to 'hold artifacts and specimens in trust for society, safeguard diverse memories for future generations and guarantee equal rights and equal access to heritage for all people' (ICOM 2019). The re-envisioned institution is acknowledged as embodying 'democratising, inclusive and polyphonic spaces for critical dialogue about the pasts and the futures' (ICOM 2019). It is precisely this aspiration of the museum to facilitate broad access and critical conversations that make it a particularly worthy focus of study in a digital era.

Museum studies scholars have referenced digitisation as defining the creation of a 'post-digital' museum and the ways in which mediatisation is intrinsic to its evolution (Parry 2013: 24). This is evidenced through what Parry (2013: 24) refers to as 'structures of legitimation' within the museum that align its goals to digital formats by embedding the digital into its exhibits and overall operations. The contemporary museum interacts with devices, platforms, screens and networks in a range of ways, transforming the space of the museum and the social encounters that take place in relation to it; however, it is distinguished from the media by its physical and material aspects (Henning 2006). This is especially important if we are to regard the museum as a 'third place' (Oldenburg 1999), an environment that sits between home and work, or public and private, where people come together both physically and digitally, and that fosters community debate. It is naïve to suggest that the institutional structures that are now scaffolded by digital media platforms remain unchanged by these alliances. Digital platforms are a means through which audiences engage with and enjoy the museum. As museums intensify their move from analogue to digital, new exhibition contexts and practices blur the boundaries between the experience of the museum and the construction of public identity by audiences on social media platforms (Wilson-Barnao 2016). What complicates matters further is the fact that museums are becoming more integrated with media platforms, which impacts how they engage with the public and operate as institutions. Platformisation and access are key notions used here for thinking through the refashioning of cultural institutions under the terms of an expanding digital economy. Media platforms are designed to maintain user interest through the production of content that renders visitor activities into data for third parties. Nieborg and Poell (2018: 1) use the term 'platformisation' to describe 'the penetration of infrastructures, economic processes and governmental frameworks of digital platforms in different economic sectors and spheres of life, as well as the reorganisation of cultural practices and imaginations around' them. The concept of museums as platforms (and its converse), thus, draws attention to the ways in which digital ecosystems contribute to the museum as a public sphere. On the one hand, museums are taking on the attributes of interactive and participatory global media platforms, which offer significant connective functions to users worldwide. On the other hand, by providing museum access, media platforms are recalibrating how the museum operates.

From this standpoint, there is a disparity between museums with transparency and accountability requirements producing cultural content versus geographies of distribution that are reliant upon commercially owned platforms and subject to different dynamics. Given the adoption of core logics that reshape these institutional structures (Dijck and Poell 2013: 2), there is a shift occurring in traditional understandings about the organisation of the museum and its visitors. This affects its characterisation as a civic environment capable of facing the challenge of acting as an inclusive space for all in a digital era and how this might align with the broader set of obligations outlined by ICOM (2019). The overall aim of this book is to present a critical appraisal of the ways in which the museum is being platformised and to explore the move towards a datafication of cultural visitors within the wider ecology of social media.

Participation, publicity and the public sphere

One example of aspects of these emerging relationships is *The Obliteration Room* by Japanese contemporary artist Yayoi Kusama, featured at the Queensland Gallery of Modern Art (QGoMA) in 2014. An installation comprising a domestic scene was constructed within the gallery, where visitors to the room were handed sheets of coloured stickers and invited to 'obliterate' by placing dots on top of everyday objects, walls and floors. Social media feeds filled in a posting frenzy throughout the summer with images of people adding colourful stickers to a white space. Visitors repeatedly recorded their on-site experiences on social media, alerting others to the exhibition in a more compelling way than any advertising campaign by making the participation of ordinary people visible. The experience of this art installation and the documentation of it via smartphone on social media acted as a highly engaging form of peer-to-peer promotion, where the engagement with the artwork by the viewer constituted the affective labour of generating sociality around the work in the gallery and then creating and circulating images of that sociality (Clough 2008). As audiences applied the adhesive dots to *The Obliteration Room* and circulated pictures on social media, they performed a type of publicity work for the institution.

This reflects a global trend towards non-traditional museums with pop-up exhibits, such as New York's Museum of Ice Cream, which encourage audiences to take photographs of their experiences and share the images on social media platforms such as Instagram. In these spaces visitors are unambiguously invited to interact with the artworks and objects by taking pictures. Similarly, Artvo, with sites in Melbourne and on the Gold Coast, describes itself on its website as a 3D 'trick art gallery' that offers visitors 'priceless photos' and 'unbelievable scenarios' (Artvo 2020). It is promoted as a 'refreshing' space where 'museum staff . . . encourage you to take as many photos and selfies as possible' (Artvo 2020). When visiting Artvo, the audience moves through different rooms expertly painted with varying scenarios. Audiences then take photos of themselves participating in the exhibit as they surf a giant wave, climb bamboo with a panda bear or enter the departure point for what resembles the train station where students enter Hogwarts in Harry Potter (see Figure 1.2).

Introduction 5

Figure 1.1 Selfie stations are a common way for museums to encourage visitors to share their experiences with social media networks, where families playfully engage with exhibits by having their picture taken.

Source: This image was taken at Adderton House & Heart of Mercy in Brisbane, Queensland, Australia.

This approach of a digitally enhanced experience that appears playful, innovative and collaborative would seem to be anathema to the traditional physical museum, embedded in serious curatorial scholarship displaying artefacts that are not meant to be touched. The contrast is illusory, as both styles of museum employ artists to paint works with which visitors interact, and that they share on social media as Instagrammable moments in an extension of their on-site meaning-making with cultural collections. Recognising the benefits of publicity, the museum has removed photography bans to encourage the online posting of audience experiences. Unsurprisingly, the traditional practices and community-building operations of the museum have adapted in parallel with the ways people build and maintain relationships online. Of course, contemporary predilections to take selfies, to post everyday minutiae and in the process publicise oneself or an organisation, are not confined to cultural institutions. Endless posting to social media, influencer culture, likes and commenting are products of the digital realm – even British Broadcasting Commission podcasts urge listeners to post on social media to 'tell others about us'. However, they serve as illustrations of how social media platforms can play a vital role in attracting audiences, sponsors and attention to the contemporary museum.

In related ways, databases of artefacts in online museum collections can create a valuable network of open data that was not previously available for audiences to engage with. In this scenario, visitors – unwittingly or not – have become adept at creating public relations value for the museum by sharing content on digital media platforms, and museums in turn increasingly understand themselves as building infrastructure that facilitates new forms of interactivity. Once they are highly ranked on internet search engines, collections can garner increased visitation both on-site and online. On the one hand, new spaces are created for user participation and interaction; on the other hand, there has been a renegotiation of the museum's role to what media scholar Jose van Dijck refers to as the 'ecosystem of connective media . . . a system that nourishes and, in turn, is nourished by social and cultural norms that simultaneously evolve in our everyday world' (van Dijck and Poell 2013: 21) (see Figure 1.2). The museum moves from being a permanent storehouse of objects to a constantly changing infrastructure where multiple publics interact, creating content, curating collections and engaging in publicity practices. In the process, audiences are imbued with enhanced visibility to the institutions and to each other, as well as contributing audience measurement services on social media sites, where the 'internet of behaviour' is able to track users in real time.

Much of the scholarship on museums is accompanied by an underlying assumption that museums will continue to provide the same level of access to their visitors. There is limited acknowledgement that recent use

Introduction 7

Figure 1.2 This illustration depicts an art exhibition that has been configured specifically for visitors to engage with using cameras and smartphones.

Source: This image was taken at Artvo on the Gold Coast, Queensland, Australia.

of digital media has impacted the museum's public orientation. Museums no longer understand themselves as exclusively providing physical access to audiences on-site. In the digital era, the provision of access to the institution involves removing photography bans so audiences can capture images of artworks, in addition to making collections available in online repositories where global audiences can play with digital objects. For example, internationally recognised expert on participation Nina Simon (2010: 2) calls for the museum to work as a 'platform that connects different users who act as content creators, distributors, consumers, critics, and collaborators'. In her view, museums can demonstrate their 'value' and 'relevance' by replicating the 'tools and design patterns' of the 'social web' that 'make participation more accessible than ever' (Simon 2010: 2). Yet, as different publics engage with the museum using smartphones or via online access, they are subject to new practices of monitoring and datafication.

Approaching the discourse of participation in the museum from this angle brings us to the distinction between publicity and the public sphere. It also provides a useful framework for understanding the contemporary museum as a domain of social life where public opinion and culture are formed. Museums have historically been institutions of the public sphere. Beyond the physical and embodied experience of the institution, a fundamental claim is that museums ought to catch up through greater mediatisation (Anderson 1999; Drotner et al. 2019). There is an inherent recognition of the need for museums to draw on digital technologies to enable broader public access to preserve and share artefacts and information. This discourse can give the impression of a radically enhanced institution, one that is more connected, participatory and democratic.

The heightened recognition of the need for digital access to collections was dramatically accelerated in 2020, following the emergence of COVID-19. For museums around the globe, the pandemic necessitated long closures as protocols around non-essential gatherings and social distancing came into play (AMGA 2020). Publicly funded institutions were forced to seek emergency funding in order to maintain jobs and operations. Private institutions without government funding, which traditionally have relied upon admission fees and donations from individuals and the private sector, were significantly impacted. In the American context, the president and CEO of the Met Museum, Daniel Weiss, explained in a media interview that institutions were operating on 'the edge, with very limited reserves. All facing unprecedented financial damage as a result of the immediate and long-term effects of the coronavirus on the economy' (Museums Association and Stephens 2020). The significant impacts of COVID-19 have forced institutions to explore new means of delivering access to collections, from livestreaming exhibition content to providing behind-the-scenes visits, through to social media engagement.

The global pandemic has revealed in a gravely acute manner the enmeshing of museums, audiences, devices and platforms. Cultural institutions educate and engage the community and are fundamentally designed to generate forms of togetherness, connection and identity. When social media and the internet are the only means through which audiences access cultural institutions, platforms play an enlarged role in generating participation and the experience of sociality. For example, on 28 January 2020, China's National Administration of Cultural Heritage asked museums to focus on online delivery of content in order to 'encourage the determination and morale of the local people to fight the epidemic and accompany all to spend a special and unforgettable Spring Festival' (Tong 2020). Institutions such as the Getty Museum in America have challenged online audiences in quarantine to recreate a work of art from their collection by using household objects and family members and then post their recreations. This has resulted in a proliferation of images of everyday people dressing up and repurposing domestic items such as toilet paper rolls, bedspreads and fruit in humorous ways to imitate famous paintings. These images are publicity outputs that promote the institution and create a sense of connection during isolation while also substituting for traditional forms of physical proximity between people and artefacts. Under COVID-19 conditions, the transformations of museums have been acute, significant and transparent, but these manifestations of change are part of a protracted and somewhat opaque radical reimagining.

Rationale, research and underlying concepts

From a societal perspective, the mediatisation of the museum raises two important questions that this book seeks to interrogate. Firstly, how have the publicity practices of visitors transformed museum access? Publicity in this sense refers to the opening up of public space as a result of increasing visibility of users who use smartphones to take photographs and curate collections online. Secondly, if cultural access is entwined with data-collection practices, what does this mean for the museum as a public sphere? To address these questions about forms of digital publicness in the museum, the critiques of public life and digital media by Mark Andrejevic (2002, 2007, 2010) and Jodi Dean (2005) are influential, and each of them aligns or responds to Jürgen Habermas's (1989) eighteenth-century conception of publicity. For Habermas, the public sphere is a space where ideal speech is realised because it is accessible to all members of the public – albeit defined as a strictly limited group of white bourgeois men. Habermas offers publicity as the practice of forming and managing public opinion. In its ideal form, critical publicity involves citizens exchanging opinions and ideas as part of a discussion that generates a consensus of opinions and attitudes, which in turn guides government. In its rational-critical form, publicity has the potential to enable an ideal symmetrical communication environment by bringing together the diverse views and opinions of multiple publics. Habermas contrasts critical publicity with manipulative publicity that re-feudalises the public sphere by distorting the public interest through covertly shaping public opinion and redirecting attention to private concerns. Within this framework, this book unpacks the way the publicity function of museums sits across a range of tensions and paradoxes with regard to its accessibility. While digital media platforms can be useful as they help the museum achieve its access imperatives, they potentially reorganise these institutions to meet the mechanisms and objectives of datafication.

The museum is a significant but often overlooked site for examining the ever-evolving dynamic among multiple publics, institutions and technology. Digital media platforms now work as conduits among users, institutions and objects in such a way that their influence on culture is not always explicit. That is not to suggest that museum visitors don't enjoy navigating the museum using mobile phones, taking photos and sharing these images on social media platforms; nor does it mean that the transformation of the museum into a more interactive and participatory environment does not come with a host of benefits – visitors can dig deeper into collections that can be accessed remotely, and experience new forms of togetherness. There is already a considerable amount of work that acknowledges these debates (Budge and Burness 2018; Rettberg 2014). In broad strokes, they hinge on questions about the different values and identities of the museum and the media and how the two are interwoven. As the title of this book suggests, the notion of digital access depends on the context surrounding how the museum is made available – that is, who owns the platform and the technologies. Digital media platforms are neither good nor bad; they are just another means by which the museum is able to achieve its mission. It is, however, necessary to recognise the influence exerted by digital media platforms over how members of the public participate. As Tarleton Gillespie (2018: 5) points out:

> The fantasy of a truly 'open' platform is powerful, resonating with deep utopian notions of community and democracy – but it is just that – a fantasy while running the risk of simultaneously integrating the museum into the wider market rationality of neoliberalism.

Accounts from within the museum

It makes sense that museum workers would seek to embrace the current practices of media platforms and draw upon digital technologies as tools to both promote the museum and make meaning with visitors. Museum workers set out with specific ideas about how they would like to provide unlimited access to collections and information available, and the extent to which audiences should be enabled to produce and consume cultural content. This book develops a behind-the-scenes account of how museum workers use digital technology to deliver access to collections, drawing on a production studies methodology (Caldwell 2008). Examples from Australia and New Zealand are used as the primary lens through which to track the adaptations occurring in the museum sector as a result of the practices of global technology companies. A production studies framework, while primarily used in film and television media context, helps to conceptualise how cultural practitioners understand their work, and in turn the evolution of the museum as a space that is undergoing significant political, economic and technological transformation. Particular kinds of mediated museum experiences are shaped by varying hierarchies of cultural workers and the narratives that play out within different communities of practice. Due to this, the perspectives of professionals working in a range of roles are equally valued for their role in the refashioning of the museum. These museum workers have much to contribute to global discussions about the spread of technology to industry practice. Historically, museums in this region have been pivoting towards digitisation since the 1970s, with a number of digital collections-management systems originating in the two countries that have been influential in the development of large online repositories (Hart and Hallett 2011). Most notably, Australian Museums Online, a searchable museum database of over 1,000 national museums and galleries, arose in the 1990s long before many other international databases of a similar nature (Chan 2020). The exhibitions and digital initiatives of museums such as MONA in Hobart, Te Papa in Wellington and QGoMA in Brisbane have international reach and significance.

This book draws upon 37 semi-structured interviews conducted with cultural professionals, including directors of cultural institutions and professionals from education, visitor studies, community engagement, social technology, market research, publicity and marketing. A visitor research analyst and academics, whose research examines the cultural sector, were also interviewed. The majority of these professionals were based in Australia and New Zealand, with a small selection of international interviewees included to obtain a broader understanding of different industry perspectives. Extracts from the anonymised accounts of these participants are considered in relation to a number of museums that are referenced as case studies. Further analysis was conducted of industry documents and communication, in particular collections of papers presented at industry conferences such as 'Museum Next' and 'Museums and the Web'. These findings were then supplemented by scrutiny of relevant industry blogs such as 'Fresh and New', 'Thinking About Museums' and 'Cultural Digital'. In addition to the interviews, fieldwork observations and documentary analysis, recent case examples have been drawn from around the globe to serve as important markers of the pace of digital transformations occurring in the museum landscape, most recently, given the impact of COVID-19. An important outcome is, therefore, the identification of how participation is employed, translated and coded into industry discussion and exhibitions and in explanations of new works.

Participation, interaction and publicity

Three concepts are critical to the way the platformisation of the museum is understood in this book. Interaction, participation and publicity are widely discussed in media studies, but they have particular meaning for and relevance to the discourse on museums and technology. Participation consists of activities that allow audiences to connect, albeit by sharing content and ideas or by creating artworks and experiences on-site and online. In contrast, interaction tends to be related specifically to technology. Participation and interaction are interlinked here because they direct our attention to changes in recent decades that have involved turning passive consumers into active prosumers (Bruns 2008). Interactive participation captures the call for asymmetrical relations with audiences within a participatory culture framework (Jenkins, Ford and Green 2013), where the authoritative structure of museums is flattened in order to facilitate enhanced audience voice. Interactive participation is entwined with publicity, which refers to the increasing visibility of ordinary people in participatory media. The concept of publicity not only builds on critiques by Jodi Dean (2002, 2010) and Mark Andrejevic (2007, 2010) of Jürgen Habermas's conceptualisation of the term but also intends to capture what Graeme Turner (2009) refers to as the 'demotic turn'. When individuals use digital devices with these spaces, they enter into an arrangement (see Figure 1.3). In exchange for making their private lives open to the monitoring capacities of digital media, they gain access to networks and the opportunities for publicity. A democratisation appears to occur as multiple publics can seemingly wield major influence, but this can result in a depoliticisation of publicness as visibility becomes commodifiable. Publicity captures the labour of audiences in producing outputs in the form of images, data and

Figure 1.3 This picture shows the Google Arts and Culture face-matching app, where users load images of themselves on an app, which are then matched with portraits resembling them housed in international museum collections.

Source: This image was produced using the Google Art and Culture App.

data trails that are interspersed into the experience of public space. Publicity is sited at the centre of museum spaces and experiences rather than forming a set of adjunct practices used to promote a museum.

Open access is a particularised understanding of the museum and its relationship with digital media practices. As most museums display less than 10 per cent of their artwork on-site, it is little wonder that many cultural workers regard technology as a tool to help the museum better engage audiences. As this book demonstrates, cultural workers increasingly theorise the museum in online terms, under the banner of common values and common good. While open access has largely been used in relation to the publication of collections as online digital repositories, the promise that is explored here in using the term 'open access' is that digital media devices and platforms are free from the obstacles inherent in traditional forms of museum access. There appears to be a preparedness to disrupt the traditional model of cultural access along with a willingness to adopt the characteristics of online platforms. There is a projection that digital media platforms work towards the same goals as the museum and that multiple publics will benefit from the increased visibility of the institution, its objects and audiences. In this sense, open access as it is used here can involve individuals sharing content, searching the internet for information, downloading apps, communicating with a chatbot, using AI and so forth. Open access promises to solve the problem of museum access by working towards the goal of providing free and innovative forms of engagement with collections but can alter the boundaries between institutions and the digital media ecosystem.

Datafication is an important concept underpinning the exploration of digital access and museums as platforms in this book. It references the technological mediation of users' daily life on digital media sites such as Netflix and Facebook, where the provision of services is reliant upon the extraction of data. Information that was once considered worthless (and that was invisible to other forms of research) is produced through the process of datafication as a form of knowledge that can be used to shape the decision-making strategies of algorithms. Datafication is a means to 'access, understand and monitor people's behaviour' (van Dijck 2014: 198), which can then be used by third parties to market goods and services. As visitors increasingly access cultural institutions using handheld devices and digital media platforms, museums have become subject to dataveillance practices. Roger Clarke (1988) expresses this as 'the systematic monitoring of people's actions or communications through the application of information technology'. Dataveillance has far-reaching implications for the museum, as the provision of free services becomes monetised through access to services (Lyon 2007).

Organisation of this book

The chapters in this book are arranged in sections according to key ideas that revolve around how cultural institutions provide digital access, both in terms of their on-site and online operations. These groupings draw on the various dimensions of the interviews and fieldwork observations that establish a context for thinking about the museum as an inclusive space where participation involves content creation and distribution on digital devices, databases and media platforms.

Chapter 2 focuses on ways in which cultural access is being extended and negotiated by museum workers. It identifies a shift in how participation assists in reorganising notions of the public's involvement and inclusion. The provision of public access is central to how museums go about making collections physically and intellectually available to current audiences. Whether privately or publicly owned, there is an inherent recognition about cultural institutions needing to preserve and share artefacts and information to broader publics. This chapter addresses ongoing attempts by the museum to function as a vehicle for communication, memory and community inclusion as it keeps pace with the emergence of new on-demand gateways for content such as Amazon and Netflix. The chapter identifies how digital media platforms can prove to be effective resources that extend the scope and reach of cultural access, while scrutinising how the terms of access are renegotiated.

Chapter 3 traces a shift from a sensory museum to the sensing museum where the physical experience of interacting with exhibits has been augmented by the use of digital technologies on-site. This involves cultural institutions moving from a mode whereby they have endeavoured to stimulate the physical senses of visitors in order to extend and share learning pedagogies to one where digital devices are used to automatically track and 'sense' how people experience an exhibit. The use of the term also captures the use of technology to stand in for the senses of visitors. The chapter concludes that the sensing museum alters traditional understandings of curation in favour of more individualised cultural experiences.

Chapter 4 deliberates on how recent shifts in the personalised use of digital devices by visitors are playing an important role in making museum content seamlessly available on digital media platforms. The aim is to consider the transformation of museum knowledge and content into a structured set of data that can easily be accessed and managed within the digital media space. Acknowledging that digital infrastructure can provide a cost-effective and convenient way of facilitating access to cultural collections, the chapter critically engages with the fundamental changes that are taking place with regard to the planning, organisation and provision of exhibitions, objects and experiences. On this basis, it reflects upon industry blogs and observations from a range of cultural professionals, who elaborate upon the efforts and activities of these institutions with regard to the digitisation of the museum.

Chapter 5 concludes by recognising the influence exerted by digital media platforms over how members of the public participate in the museum. There are complex dynamics and tensions associated with private platforms facilitating and moderating access to the field of culture and cultural production. As museums integrate digital media devices and platforms into their programming, architecture and engagement strategies, they adapt to the logics of publicity and monitoring that are central to the new media economy. The data generated through the use of digital devices produce commercial value for both the institution and the media platforms. For museums, audience data generate nuanced public relations, marketing and personalisation strategies. For media platforms, audience documentation of the museum experience arguably delivers important cultural information about often-valuable taste-making consumers. A different iteration of private/public institution is proposed as having emerged, whereby cultural access is facilitated within the parameters of a digital ecosystem that sees economic influence being exerted indirectly through forms of data capture and analysis. A key thread of the argument in this book is that one of the seminal features of the contemporary museum that differentiates it from earlier modes of curation and display is the extension of platform media into the field of culture and cultural production. This has been brought into sharp relief with the global COVID-19 pandemic, which has provided a lens through which to briefly discuss responses by museums to this crisis, but then situate this conversation in the longer arc of change in the museum as a public sphere.

References

Anderson, Maxwell (1999). Museums of the future: The impact of technology on museum practices. *Daedalus*, 3: 128–62.
Andrejevic, Mark (2007). *iSpy: Surveillance and Power in the Interactive Era*. Lawrence, KS: University Press of Kansas.
Andrejevic, Mark (2010). Reading the surface: Body language and surveillance. *Culture Unbound: Journal of Current Cultural Research*, 2(1): 15–36.
Artvo (2020). About Artvo. Retrieved from www.artvo.com.au.
Australian Museums and Galleries Association (AMGA) (2020). *Covid-19 Reopening and Recovery Hub for Museums and Galleries*. Australian Museums and Galleries Association. Retrieved from www.amaga.org.au/covid19-reopening-and-recovery-hub-museums-and-galleries.
Bennett, Tony (1998). Pedagogic objects, clean eyes, and popular instruction: On sensory regimes and museum didactics. *Configurations*, 6(3): 345–71.
Blakenberg, N. and Lord, G. D. (2015). *Cities, Museums and Soft Power*. Washington, DC: AAM Press.
Bruns, Axel (2008). *Wikipedia, Second Life, and Beyond: From Production to Produsage*. New York: Peter Lang.
Budge, Kylie and Burness, Alli (2018). Museum objects and Instagram: Agency and communication in digital engagement. *Continuum*, 32(2): 137–50.
Caldwell, John T. (2008). *Production Culture, Industrial Reflexivity and Critical Practice in Film and Television*. Durham, NC: Duke University Press.

Chan, Seb (2020). 57. Looking backwards to go forwards, words from talks. *Fresh and New*. Retrieved from https://sebchan.substack.com/p/57-looking-backwards-to-go-forwards.
Clarke, Roger (1988). Information technology and dataveillance. *Communications of the ACM*. Retrieved from https://dl.acm.org/doi/abs/10.1145/42411.42413.
Clough, Patricia T. (2008). The affective turn: Political economy, bio media and bodies. *Theory, Culture & Society*, 25(1): 1–22.
Dean, Jodi (2002). *Publicity's Secret: How Technoculture Capitalizes on Democracy*. New York: Cornell University Press.
Dean, Jodi (2005). Communicative capitalism: Circulation and the foreclosure of politics. *Cultural Politics*, 1(1): 51–74.
Dean, Jodi (2010). Affective networks. *Media Tropes eJournal*, 2(2): 19–44.
Drotner, Kirsten, Dziekan, Vince, Parry, Ross and Christian, Kim (2019). *The Routledge Handbook of Museums, Media and Communication*. London: Routledge.
Gillespie, Tarleton (2018). *Custodians of the Internet: Platforms, Content Moderation, and the Hidden Decisions that Shape Social Media*. New Haven, CT: Yale University Press.
Habermas, Jürgen (1989). *The Structural Transformation of the Public Sphere*. (Trans. T. Burger and F. Lawrence). Cambridge MA: The MIT Press.
Heath and Von Lehn, 2009.
Hart, Tim and Hallett, Martin (2011). Australian museums and the technology revolution. In Des Griffin and Leon Paroissien (eds), *Understanding Museums*. Canberra: National Museum Australia. Retrieved from https://nma.gov.au/research/understanding-museums/THart_MHallett_2011.html.
Henning, Michelle (2006). *Museums, Media and Cultural Theory*. New York: Open University Press.
Henning, Michelle (2017). Museum media: An introduction. In Kylie Message and Andrea Witcomb (eds), *The International Handbooks of Museum Studies*, Vol. 2. London: John Wiley & Sons, pp. xlii–lix.
International Council of Museums (ICOM) 2019. Museum definition. Retrieved from https://icom.museum/en/resources/standards-guidelines/museum-definition.
Jenkins, Henry, Ford, Sam and Green, Joshua (2013). *Spreadable Media*. New York: New York University Press.
Lyon, David (2007). *Theorizing Surveillance: The Panopticon and Beyond*. Cullompton: Willan.
Museums Association and Simon Stephens (2020). *Coronavirus: What Impact is the Pandemic Having on Museums Worldwide?* London: Museums Association. Retrieved from www.museumsassociation.org/museums-journal/news/2020/03/26032020-coronavirus-pandemic-worldwide-impact-museums.
Nieborg, David and Poell, Thomas (2018). The platformisation of cultural production: Theorizing the contingent cultural commodity. *New Media & Society*, 20(11): 4275–92.
Oldenburg, Ray (1999). *The Great Good Place: Cafes, Coffee Shops, Bookstores, Bars, Hair Salons, and Other Hangouts at the Heart of a Community*. New York: Hachette.

Parry, Ross (2013). The end of the beginning: Normativity in the postdigital museum. *Museum Worlds: Advances in Research*, 1(1): 24–39.

Rettberg, Jill W. (2014). *Seeing Ourselves Through Technology: How We Use Selfies, Blogs and Wearable Devices to See and Shape Ourselves*. Basingstoke: Palgrave Macmillan.

Simon, Nina (2010). *The Participatory Museum*. Santa Cruz, CA: Creative Commons. Retrieved from www.participatorymuseum.org.

Tong, Yaoi (2020). How Chinese museums are coping with coronavirus: An in-depth report. *The Art Newspaper*, 4 March. Retrieved from www.theartnewspaper.com/analysis/behind-closed-doors-how-museums-in-china-are-coping-with-coronavirus.

Turner, Graeme (2009). *Ordinary People and the Media: The Demotic Turn*. Thousand Oaks, CA: Sage.

van Dijck, Jose (2014). Datafication, dataism and dataveillance: Big data between scientific paradigm and ideology. *Surveillance & Society*, 12(2): 197–208.

van Dijck, Jose and Poell, Thomas (2013). Understanding social media logic. *Media and Communication*, 1(1): 2–14.

Wilson-Barnao, Caroline (2016). The personalization of publicity in the museum. *Continuum*, 30(6): 688–96.

Wilson-Barnao, Caroline (2017). How algorithmic cultural recommendations influence the marketing of cultural collections. *Consumption, Markets & Culture*, 20(6): 559–74.

Wilson-Barnao, Caroline (2018). The logic of platforms: How 'on demand' museums are adapting in the digital era. *Critical Arts*, 32(3): 1–16.

Wilson-Barnao, Caroline (2020). The quantified and customised museum. *Public*, 30(60): 208–19.

Witcomb, Andrea (2003). *Re-imagining the Museum: Beyond the Mausoleum*. New York: Routledge.

2 The logic of open access to culture

Introduction

Touching Masterpieces, an innovative project by NeuroDigital Technologies, based in Spain, and the National Gallery of Prague, was launched in late 2018 (Springwise 2018). It harnesses the vibratory and tactile senses of VR haptic gloves paired with virtual 3D scans of some well-known sculptures (NeuroDigital Technologies 2020). College student David Stein, who has sight impairment caused by damage to his visual cortex in a car accident as a child, took part in the immersive experience. These technological advances are life-changing for him, as he seeks to major in ancient history and anthropology but was concerned about his preferred choice of study, given that his visual access to cultural objects is limited. This immersive experience provided David with the opportunity to touch, feel and create an image of a statue of Nefertiti from a 3D scan that afforded him a different way of seeing.

Technology companies and cultural institutions partnered in these ways can render transformations in access to the millions of people globally who are blind or visually impaired, thus opening up access to world cultural treasures to wider and more diverse audiences. Clearly, further research and development are required to refine the digital devices, reduce the costs and ensure enhanced availability to users and to artefacts; yet the pace of change is already significant.

For David, this feels like a good step in the right direction and he is excited, but he also wonders whether the technology will be available widely, with sufficient scans made public or openly accessible to make it worthwhile for him to own these gloves himself. While David is a fictional character, he serves to highlight the technology, its benefits and limitations. How can museums use technology to guide and provide access in the future? To appreciate the scope of this question, it is essential to clarify 'access' in contrast to 'open access', as both are central to how cultural institutions

DOI: 10.4324/9780429298691-2

understand their relationship with multiple audiences. Being open versus being accessible represent differing notions but they are interrelated and reflect their construction within specific historical and ideological formations of public institutions.

Access, interactivity/participation and publicity are core features of the platformisation of museums. The provision of access is used to explain how the museum understands its civic function and refers to how it made itself available to its multiple publics. The idea of, and focus on, access developed when the museum moved from the princely collections to public collections of the nation-state and the developing framework for access was used to capture the evolving intellectual and infrastructural concerns of these institutions and how they straddle collecting, research and engagement. In contrast, open access developed as a response to the recent amalgamation of the internet and other sensory devices, such as the smartphone, into the practices of research and collecting repositories. It is commonly defined as making all outputs freely available via the internet, permitting any user to read, download, copy, distribute, print, search or link without financial, legal or technical barriers. Tim Sherratt (2019: 119) sketches how online interfaces 'make assumptions about the needs and desires of users. They do not merely provide access; they construct it by defining the types of interactions we can have with collections.' In this way, 'digital infrastructures decide what should be hidden from view or prioritised based upon a range of factors which can perpetuate historic assumptions and prejudices'.

This chapter builds upon research by Wiedemann, Patzschke and Schmitt (2019: 193) on German museums and how museum workers justify the digital transformation of collections as a direct response to an enhanced call for open access. Agreeing with the perspective that museum workers are adopting different practices and strategies to respond to a perceived need for digital transformation, it argues that platformisation and access are interrelated.

Reviewing the history of access helps us to understand how the emergent shift towards using internet tools as norms of practice by both the public and the museum impacts the cultural institutions. Having identified past formations, new strategies of mediatised open access are explored and compared. The reflections of museum workers, academic literature and a selection of industry documents are melded together to canvass the similarities and differences in the frameworks that underpin the delivery of cultural access.

This approach makes it possible to examine some of the normalised assumptions of museum workers regarding the adoption of open access principles and approaches to the delivery of exhibition content, while the aim is to get a clear sense of the ethical frameworks that underpin contemporary access and to build upon understandings about how museums see themselves using digital technology to enhance collection access. This furthers the examination of the evolving and constructed character of cultural access within museum environments.

By identifying key themes and dwelling on the different understandings of access, both past and present, the chapter seeks to understand the variety of perceptions and priorities that cultural workers hold and the extent to which these approaches shape how collections are experienced, both now and in the future. The next section first attempts to articulate the historic role of access to collections before moving to define open access in relation to the museum. Having distinguished access from open access, the chapter then considers how open access sets the groundwork for the creation of 'labs' that construct accessibility technologies and new ways of working for museums.

Making sense of access

An evolutionary aspect of public museums is that their collections arose from the church and the princely private collections of the wealthy, which were not available for public viewing. Tony Bennett (1995: 24) suggests that it was not until the mid- to late-nineteenth century that the museum began to be regarded as a governmental institution characterised by three core attributes:

> First, it was a social space where codes of behaviour previously associated with other spaces of public assembly, became enforced as appropriate practices of public conduct. Second, it was a space of self-improvement and education. And third it was a space of observation and regulation.

The state made its riches available to visitors who, with equal access, had the power to improve themselves as a result of the encounter. This required a conscious transformation of these spaces from private domains to physical and intellectual spaces available to the whole population. Thus museums were imbued with, and encouraged, a specific state of 'middle-class' habits, morals, values and beliefs, and they did this by guiding visitors to what to see and how to see it. This also demonstrated to these audiences how to 'see' each other (Bennett 1995: 52).

Defining the new museum

This defined the museum as a space where the working classes were allegedly 'lifted up' by access to 'the improving influence of the middle classes' and by the civilising influence of women as 'culture's gentle handmaidens'

(Bennett 1995: 28–29). In making government collections available, public visitors were welcomed to view collections in which they had a stake. Women were also brought into the space of the institution as a civilising force that would shape the conduct of men, who would then pay attention to maintaining proper standards of behaviour in response to their presence. Viewed from this perspective, the museum acted as a public sphere that theoretically welcomed everyone, provided they abided by the rules (Bennett 1995). Bennett (1995: 9) delineates this as a shift towards a 'parity of representation' by these institutions and recognition that 'all social groups should have equal practical as well as theoretical rights of access to museums'.

This isn't to say that museums have always provided equal access to all people. Without doubt, by their very nature, they are cultural formations that order objects into taxonomies that conform with the broader cultural and historical ideas. This conception of access is derived from a western-centric perspective, as the collections held in museums were not always 'given' with 'informed consent by their Indigenous owners, nor were they spaces where the traditional owners of those artifacts were welcomed' (Christen 2012: 2876). The museum could serve as a welcoming space for all people, but it still assumed an authoritative stance. Access to culture facilitated 'by the high for the low' and the masses were guided with regard to what to think and do (Weil 2002: 258). Access existed more as an idea that was used to promote and propagate a particular type of citizen who benefited from access to state-owned collections.

The late 1970s and early 1980s are now broadly acknowledged as the decade when a fresh body of museum scholarship emerged with a different perspective on the museum as a public sphere. Prompted by a public perception of the museum as elitist, the 'new museology' arose in response to a desire for heightened community participation in cultural experiences (Vergo 1989). A range of factors are credited with disrupting these old ways of thinking. In particular, static or reduced government funding created an impetus to compete for audiences, publicity and resources. Audience access was a central concern, as it forced museums to acknowledge their authoritative structures and consider ways to reconfigure their practices to attract marginalised groups or audiences who were at risk of being excluded.

The concept of public good was linked to the use of public money and carried important managerial implications. Museums were regarded as beneficial to the well-being of multiple publics because 'by definition' they were 'accessible to everyone' and were able to 'function as especially clear demonstrations of the state's commitment to equality', making 'visible the public it claims to serve' (Duncan 1991: 93). As a consequence, access worked as a guiding principle that allowed the museum to clearly demonstrate the quality of its relationships with the community and government funding bodies. The emphasis of public good and public value (Scott 2010: 34) emerged in Britain in the 1980s and 1990s as a way for public institutions in particular to evaluate and explain the importance of their contribution to government. Richard Sandell (1998) suggests the widespread adoption of the term 'social exclusion' derived from New Labour in the United Kingdom, further reinforcing the need for museums to demonstrate their social purpose and broad community access.

The mixture of meanings associated with social exclusion, public good and public value was linked to a view of publicly funded museums as stewards of public assets. This dictated that publicly owned museums in particular worked towards being considerate and inclusive as possible of their communities and individual visitor requirements in terms of their buildings, processes, exhibitions and operations. Western institutions endeavoured to demonstrate their value to avoid 'closure, staff redundancy and the introduction of entrance fees' in an environment of diminished public sector investment (Jafari, Taheri and vom Lehn 2013). This doesn't suggest that access was (or is) solely the concern of state museums, but instead highlights that the idea took root primarily in relation to institutions funded by the public purse. The provision of 'equal access to all', whether manifested as access to services, information, buildings or employment, along with making opportunities available for people to 'participate in decision making' became a key concern (Australian Museum 2014).

The term 'access' incorporated infrastructural concerns such as wheelchair ramps and Braille text right through to free exhibitions and affordable ticket pricing. Therefore, 'access' was used to capture how the museum engaged with the community (despite variations in operational and funding capacity) via its collections, educational programming, public engagement and research infrastructure. Collections undeniably contribute to public knowledge and well-being, and as a result demand accessibility to all people, to evince value for the population supporting the government of the day. Certainly not equally applied by all museums, there is a clear relationship between the set of values and relations that underpin 'parity of representation' and the idea of access in its current imagining.

Strategically, museums work towards confronting and exploring their complex histories and make efforts to involve communities in collection description and display. Access to museum collections and resources is understood as a basic right for all citizens. Access remains an important priority for most institutions and often involves considerations that can be physical, cultural, social, intellectual, attitudinal and financial, ranging from opening times, wheelchair ramps, toilets and philosophical assumptions to easy-to-understand language on labels and familiar concepts. This approach holds the museum accountable for considering the power differential between visitors and staff, and recognises that, rather than being a final destination, access requires continual improvement.

The Museums Association, a professional body with over 10,000 members, provides a code of ethics that was developed in response to ICOM's definition of museum (see ICOM 2019), as it relates to the delivery of access. Central to this understanding is the view that museums have a public service orientation. It states:

> Museums belong to everybody. They exist to serve the public. They should enhance the quality of life of everyone, both today and in the future. They are funded because of their positive social, cultural, educational and economic impact.
>
> (Museums Association 2002)

The concept and framework of access guide an institution's decision-making with regard to the community and pay attention to the inclusivity of its interpretation, education, exhibition, outreach and research practices. A quick Google search of museum websites produces a long list of statements about the delivery of access and pre-trip information. Accessibility maps with information relating to entrances, parking, wheelchair accessible toilets, lifts and amenities are designed to enhance the visitor experience and are provided by most institutions. Access is articulated on websites to audiences as a means of providing information to visitors with specific access requisites.

Importantly, the provision of access was identified by nearly all the people interviewed for this book as fundamental to the museum's core purpose as a public space. An acting director of a major Australian state gallery and museum carefully described the importance of access and outlined the different areas in which the museum has endeavoured to make itself available to various publics:

> Access in museums is what we are all after, but it is a complicated thing: ramps, Braille and computer terminals do not equal access in museums. It is more, far more: intellectual access, social access and physical access. Access for me is understanding your audiences and then meeting an audience's communication needs. . . . Social access can often require something much bigger than the museum itself because many people who don't visit museums simply don't have the idea within their own paradigm of possible leisure or learning options.

As this description highlights, even though centuries have passed since the museum's move from princely to public collections, it remains remarkably intent on providing access. The idealised access articulated by this cultural professional is echoed in the reflections of other professionals interviewed in the course of this research. An engagement manager at a prominent Australian library explained access by emphasising the different channels of audience engagement it can leverage:

> We have four pillars in our strategy that we use to think about access. But access is multifaceted and I don't think that we should take that linear view. So we think about visitor experience onsite and we think about visitor experience online but those experiences are multidimensional. That is interesting because I wonder if that thinking reflects the structure of how the organisation works. There might be an opportunity to restructure slightly differently, with different accountabilities cutting across.

The language that cultural workers use to describe access matters and it reflects the conscious choices made by institutions and their employees. These two reflections demonstrate ideologies about how to engage audiences and are primarily grounded in efforts to expand access and the provision of meaning-making opportunities for visitors. However, the approach to the delivery of access differs and is specific to the collection, audience and institutional capacities.

Some museum workers felt it was important to use a range of different technologies and approaches to communicating with audiences. An audience engagement manager at a leading New Zealand museum stressed this perspective, explaining that 'there are times for the museum voice but more and more there needs to be different voices'. Access, as it is described here, extends beyond the frame of the physical institution or its website but is regarded as something that can be improved upon when opened up to a broader cultural voice.

Always creating new opportunities for audience engagement is central to how the museum understands itself. What is poignant about the first director's reflection is the account of access that captures the social desires of visitors. The museum is a place where visitors see themselves represented and are able to participate in multiple modes of discourse. This was captured by another interviewee, who said, 'There is no sign saying "don't do anything!"' In this sense, access seeks out what is missing and works towards finding a range of strategies to overcome obstacles that prevent people from engaging with collections. It is a space for dialogue and of social exchange. It is a children's play area, pram parking, free Wi-Fi and so on (see Figure 2.1). Access is the visible (and invisible) set of values that underpin museum operations. Both access and open access are not easily

Figure 2.1 The museum works towards making itself available to multiple publics through the provision of welcoming spaces. This picture depicts pram parking outside a children's activity corner.

Source: This photo was taken at a Queensland cultural institution.

rendered to the satisfaction of all, however. In 2019 over '75 New York art galleries' were served 'with lawsuits alleging' violation of 'the Americans With Disabilities Act (ADA) because their websites are not equally accessible to blind and visually impaired consumers' (Kinsella 2019).

Defining open access

Initially evolving out of the sharing of academic journals and research, the idea of open access arose as a guiding principle in the 1990s in line with the evolution of the internet. The term 'open access' refers to making publicly funded content freely available using digital means, and access captures the dissemination of content via the internet where users can download and share information, including the idea of Creative Commons. Open access closely aligns with the values of publicly funded museum, but in its first iteration was designed to support the transition of new forms of content onto the internet.

The Budapest Open Access Initiative of 2001 and the Berlin Declaration on 'Open Access to Knowledge in the Sciences and Humanities' in 2003 were pivotal points in generating a shared understanding about how open access should be operationalised (Wiedemann, Patzschke and Schmitt 2019). This interpretation was related to a growing belief that there were direct benefits from rearranging how people thought about access. The overall aim was for content and metadata to be made broadly available on the internet and for it to be used, reused and distributed freely by users. Immediate access via the internet and shareability, regardless of public and corporate use, were key (Berlin 9 2011).

Significantly, the Public Sector Information Directive, which was put in place in 2003 by the European Union, contains guidelines to address the economic aspects of information-sharing and expanded in 2013 to capture research and cultural infrastructures such as museums (Wiedemann, Patzschke and Schmitt 2019: 194). Only a few years before, in 2010, the Open GLAM initiative was also formed as a branch of the 'Open Knowledge Foundation'. This group was important because it argued that 'Galleries, Libraries, Archives & Museums (GLAMs)' should 'realise the full potential of the internet for access, innovation and digital scholarship' (Open GLAM 2019). The Open GLAM initiative set out to clearly define the use of open access in the context of cultural institutions. It articulated requirements for anyone to 'freely access, use, modify, and share for any purpose' works held in cultural repositories. This initiated and enabled a move towards overcoming some of the limitations of copyright and intellectual property before content can be released.

In other words, the general call for open access suggests that, where possible, knowledge-based institutions should not withhold collection content and should strive towards a notion of 'openness'. By sharing high-quality digital reproductions, cultural organisations work towards opening up the availability of their collections while controlling the quality of the related images circulated on the internet. The museum relinquishes its rights of ownership by allowing commercial and non-commercial entities to use these digital reproductions of copyright-free material for their own purposes. The public can then distribute and modify content without fear of litigation. This perspective has been operationalised by online collections such as Europeana and the Rijksmuseum, which not only share high-quality images but also have linked open data. This means that metadata for objects can be downloaded freely using public Application Programming Interfaces (APIs). The metadata comprise downloadable files or snippets that make images and information recognisable to computers.

Licensed under the Creative Commons Zero (CC0), a public domain dedication tool that relinquishes copyright, museums then release content.

GitHub Repositories are also used as a way to store and make broadly available source code for projects, files and changes to programming. While creating API and GitHub Repositories can cost institutions considerable staff time and expense, some cultural institutions see great advantage in this approach.

In an attempt to define the values that underpin the development of data use by cultural institutions the 'Santa Barbara Statement on Collections as Data' was formed in 2017 by the Institute of Museum and Library Services at Collections as Data National Forum in Santa Barbara, California. Acknowledging the benefits of using computational methods to extend access, the formation of the 'Santa Barbara Statement' signalled a shared intention to shift the practices of the sector towards open formats and open data (Always Already Computational 2017). It is noteworthy that the majority of definitions and examples of open access on websites implicitly and explicitly identify the rationale behind the benefits of applying open access principles to museum environments, which then replicate the values outlined in the 'Santa Barbara Statement'. Working explicitly as a code of conduct, this statement underscores the importance of new opportunities to engage audiences using computational methods to share collections, workflows, data sheets, code books, provenance and so forth, unless ethical or legal issues impinge upon the openness of this content (Always Already Computational 2017).

The former director of digital departments at the San Francisco Museum of Modern Art (MoMA), Keir Winesmith, co-authored a blog post with Anna Carey in 2014 and explained the reason for using APIs:

> Museums are primarily outward-facing institutions, a characteristic that becomes the foundation for everything the museum does. Museums also are homes to massive amounts of data: about their physical objects, people involved at the institution, their programming, and their history. At their core, most museums cohere perfectly with the current trend in open data, which is about making data available and usable to the broadest possible audience. A museum's API has the potential to do just this.
>
> (Winesmith and Carey 2014)

This explanation demonstrates that obstacles to sharing are sought out and overcome in order to make collections more adaptable and useful. Collection APIs are interpreted as a space for innovation and discovery, which allows the museum to establish itself as an interactive component of contemporary digital life.

By enabling software to communicate findings, data can be examined for new purposes, including building apps and creating novel projects. The

Cleveland Museum of Art in the United States identifies the benefits of open access to its collection and Microsoft (2020) features a video on its website highlighting that open access makes it possible to 'create and transform your experience through art . . . for the benefit of all people forever'. This short statement identifies the broad idea behind open access, indicating that there are long-term benefits from the reuse of cultural content held in central repositories, both in terms of the enlarged visibility of collections and broader user engagement.

Common formats, shared workflows and industry standards are regarded as key to opening cultural institutions to new audiences and to the museum supporting the development of research. Australian industry leader Seb Chan of the Australian Centre for the Moving Image (ACMI) in Melbourne, formerly from the Cooper Hewitt in New York City, in a 2019 Medium blog titled 'Fire, Fire, Fire – Words from a Creative State', describes the core of his work for the past decade as based upon a 'principle of openness', which he characterises as scaffolding 'a web-native, web-scale institution' with 'deliberate design and infrastructural choices'. This largely involves getting museums to use 'open access, open source and open APIs' (Chan 2019). By making content available through APIs, with their associated metadata, collections stimulate new forms of research, interrogation and analysis, including AI's searching for meaning, facial recognition and mining billions of points of data. Collection data can also be used to create new outputs that can encourage fresh forms of engagement.

GLAM labs: Their development and importance

Over the past decade, GLAM labs have spread globally in response to numerous organisations looking to share and experiment with data and collections. GLAM labs are a group or department within cultural heritage institutions responsible for the digitisation of maps, music, photographs and manuscripts, 3D virtual objects and even the archiving of sound recordings of machines, tribal music, old TV programs and video games from the 1980s (Mahey et al. 2019). Developing these technologies creates the possibility for greater audience access and participation, regardless of the collection differences and varying technical complexities. Initially originating from the library sector and expanding into other museum and gallery sectors, GLAM labs are primarily non-commercial in their orientation but can be physical or virtual spaces aimed at bringing together people, institutions and technology for the purpose of reimagining how to make collections accessible. These labs encourage cultural workers to collaborate and innovate using technology. This can often involve sharing code, information or ideas online that museum workers perceive as beneficial to other parties.

As a result, GLAM labs have also been instrumental in driving awareness for cultural institutions to make available open data in order to extend collection access. In doing so, these cross-disciplinary collectives make viable the long-term staffing implications for the museum. A group of experts working globally in the cultural sector recently published an online book titled *Open a Glam Lab* (2019), in which they proposed the following definition:

> A (GLAM) lab is a place for experimenting with digital collections and data. It is where researchers, artists, entrepreneurs, educators and the interested public can collaborate with an engaged group of partners to create new collections, tools, and services that will help transform the future ways in which knowledge and culture are disseminated. The exchanges and experimentation in a lab are open, iterative and shared widely.
>
> (Mahey et al. 2019: 31)

There is no question that this explanation describes a shared space that is built upon a model where collections are broadly distributed via the internet. This focused innovation from the sector provides an important driver to invest in systems and networks that extend the institution's digital infrastructure.

Such models represent an enhanced collaborative approach to sharing cultural content that potentially challenges the traditional power structures of the museum. However, there isn't necessarily the same level of understanding across institutional departments about what the provision of open access entails. A digital engagement manager at a large Australian state art museum explained:

> When I started [with the organisation] we had a strategy. We are going to be the virtual museum and it's like okay, why? So then I started going around getting everyone to express what that meant. What it meant actually wasn't very clear. So people thought we would get consultants to create a model of the gallery. Others thought we would get flythroughs or walk throughs – so people could see what the gallery looks like over the internet. Others (in horror) thought that is not what we need people to do with the art!

Museum workers often have intersecting perspectives about the requirement for the institution to be 'out there', but there is a concomitant lack of clarity about what 'being out there' actually entails.

Recognition of the necessity to adapt to some of the innovations is modelled and publicised by larger institutions that have more developed open access policies. The same museum professional went on to explain:

> And you can look to others in the sector that are doing some really interesting things. Like the Rijksmuseum in Amsterdam, Cleveland Art Museum with Gallery One in the US and they have done really ground breaking things while their buildings have been closed.

Perhaps unsurprisingly, almost one-third of the participants interviewed conflated open access with other forms of access. Issues such as copyright and protocols for consultation were highlighted as important considerations. Many practitioners recognised that access to the physical institution could operate independently of its online avatar. An education and audience research manager at a large Australian state-based museum explained:

> You can have access by having elements of our collection on our website that people can see. And we do. We have a vast amount of our collection that is on the website, so those things allow access which is independent of interactivity . . . that kind of digital world, they can be quite independent of each other potentially.

The research underpinning this book identified a sense that the museum needs to accept a loss of control over the use of its content, at least to a certain extent, if artefacts are to 'gain a new life'. This can be a source of conflict between different departments within the same institution, and there can be varying perspectives and desires about the extent to which the museum should express authority over how an artefact is used online. The exploitation of cultural content from Indigenous collections is a prime concern that highlights these tensions (Singh and Blake 2012). However, the values around access to collections remains pervasive to the extent that most of the cultural workers interviewed acknowledged that a lessening of control over the use of collection content was necessary and preferable to a lack of online engagement with the institution.

By creating avenues for interaction with content, museums demonstrate the contemporary relevance of collections with online audiences. A museum manager digital services at an Australian state museum acknowledged the need for the museum to talk with its visitors using different technologies and provided an example of a popular Flickr commons photograph from a museum collection of a skeleton that had self-evolved into a game (see Figure 2.2). By placing a mouse cursor over the online image,

32 *The logic of open access to culture*

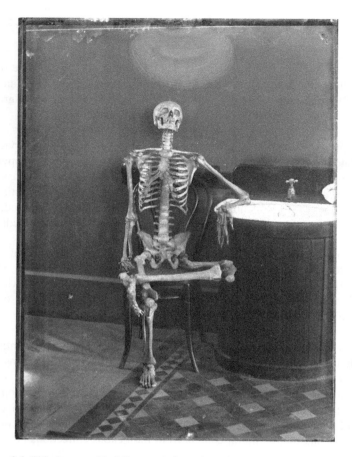

Figure 2.2 This image, titled *Portrait of an Articulated Skeleton on a Bentwood Chair* (c. 1900) is in the Powerhouse Museum collection on Flickr and was a gift of the estate of Raymond W. Phillips (2008). It has been viewed 1,072,037 times, with 4,292 favs and 588 comments with users playfully engaging with the image by tagging and commenting.

Source: Image courtesy of the Powerhouse Museum, public domain via Wikimedia Commons.

audiences sought out free space among the hundreds of posts by different users where they could add a comment of their own. The photograph was repurposed to generate a new form of collective engagement.

Digitisation also enables a cost-effective means of broadening access to collections. Experiences like the participatory photo of the skeleton allow access because people learn about a collection, experience objects and

The logic of open access to culture 33

interact with each other at the same time. Due to this, digital objects can appear more 'democratic' because users are 'prosumers' (Ritzer and Jurgenson 2010), who share their ideas and creations and are given the opportunity to engage in conversations. Similar to Habermas's (1989) depiction of critical publicity, the museum is repurposed within media platforms as a space where co-created readings and meanings can be exchanged. This exposes both copyright and knowledge implications, and means that the museum's traditional remit as an authoritative custodian is disrupted.

Competing views of access and open access coexist, and there are points of intersection and difference between the understandings expressed by the cultural professionals working within these environments. As Taco Dibbits, Rijksmuseum director of collections, announced when the institution made 125,000 artworks freely available in high resolution in 2013: 'If they want to have a Vermeer on their toilet paper, I'd rather have a very high-quality image of Vermeer on toilet paper than a very bad reproduction' (Segal 2013). Here, the museum director characterises museum visitors not through the physical space of the institution but as viewers, creators and consumers who engage with the museum collection not only for play but also for commerce (see Figure 2.3). This adjustment is largely related to the adoption of the CC0 by the museum, which allows users to repurpose work and distribute it without concern for litigation.

Figure 2.3 Museum visitor photographing 'Say cheese please, but they can't'.

Source: Nachtwacht / Nightwatch, Rembrandt van Rijn, Rijksmuseum Amsterdam Netherlands" by PAUL (Van de Velde) -Fotografie is licensed with CC BY 2.0. To view a copy of this license, visit https://creativecommons.org/licenses/by/2.0/

The benefit of these technologies is that they can make artworks that are physically difficult for users to access more available and interactive. Digital access can foster curiosity and deepen audience engagement through the creation of new spaces where museum visitors can express their creativity by collecting, curating and sharing artworks. This adds pressure on museums to embrace new technologies and to use them to supplement collection access. The largest art museum in the United States and a leader in open access, the Metropolitan Museum of Art, now has over 375,000 images available online under CC0 (The Met 2017). While these collections effectively expand public experience of the original artwork, there are tensions associated with this approach. On the Met's website Artstor, the Digital Public Library of America, Wikimedia and Pinterest are among the partners listed in the initiative (The Met 2017).

Flickr, the photo-sharing site that at its peak had over 90 million users, was sold by Yahoo in 2018 due to concerns about its financial viability. It has since pivoted to align itself with the museum sector by removing free user accounts and providing storage and sharing for over 120 public institutions, which include the Smithsonian, the Rijksmuseum and the US National Archives (Flickr 2019). Only time and further commercialisation will tell whether this improves the site's financial viability.

Of the professionals interviewed, most acknowledged that digital media platforms were extending their sphere of influence as intermediaries of cultural content. Some expressed concerns about who was collecting, downloading and possibly misusing cultural content using digital means (and for what purpose), while more often it was deemed imperative to release collection content to a broader public. Open access was mostly imagined as a democratising force that moved the institution away from a more elitist format. The visitor becomes more interactive and participatory while simultaneously linked with the media system. This is paradoxical, as the ability of the museum to sustain its audience reach becomes reliant on the agility of the public who utilise media platforms and who are adept at using digital tools, including apps and devices. Digital replicas of artefacts become part of the flow of everyday life.

Conclusion

On the basis of the material presented in this chapter, the perceptions of access articulated by cultural workers cannot be characterised as 'set' but instead reflect a set of standards and morals that they negotiate daily with regard to making the museum available to its multiple publics. While at times articulations of 'access' shift, the notion is used predominantly to describe the museum creating social inclusion and political unity. This approach is baked into the views of government-funded museums in order to demonstrate that their spaces and assets are inclusive and widely used by the public and that they must be seen to lead the sector. In this way, the museum invited the community into a more equal relationship, where members contributed to collective decision-making (Scott 2010). The museum's programming and values have had to align with those of the public in order to champion the institutions' cause to government, which in turn helped to secure funding (Scott 2010; Weil 2002).

Continuing previous precedents for public involvement, exhibitions are now explored and shared by online communities. Cultural workers often balance the usability of collections online against unintended audience uses of digital artefacts. Rather than being outside looking in, the public experiences an augmented and open configuration of an institution with its objects arranged to accommodate the call for new forms of digital participation and interaction. There is a sense that visitors will be emotionally engaged with the museum if they interact with its content. This same interaction, then, evidences a blended acknowledgement of public value, which is ported from past understandings of museum access. However, in contrast with the previous decade, museums are no longer consistently the sole architects of the infrastructure that delivers access to collections. Media platforms now work as a conduit that appears to guarantee the museum's extension as a ubiquitous public space, shifting how the institution delivers collection access.

The imaginings of an intelligent and responsive museum as evidenced in this chapter, to become one that is able to dynamically adapt as a responsive and changing environment are in many ways coming to fruition. To provide access to the museum, the institution must implicitly understand the visitor and think and learn from each and every visit. In this scenario, there is a dramatic altering of the way the museum operates by drawing on forms of algorithmic intelligence aimed at consistently improving visitor access and experience by tracking and predicting artefacts based on visitor navigation. There is a porting of the protocols and practices of media platforms into the physical space of the museum through the enactment of personalisation to enhance and capture the sensing experiences of audiences; this is discussed in the next chapter.

References

Always Already Computational (2017). The Santa Barbara statement on collections as data. Retrieved from https://collectionsasdata.github.io/statement.
Australian Museum (2014). Accessibility and inclusion. Retrieved from https://australian.museum/about/organisation/reports/accessibility-inclusion-action-plan.

Bennett, Tony (1995). *The Birth of the Museum: History, Theory, Politics*. London: Routledge.

Berlin 9 (2011). The Berlin declaration on open access. Berlin 9 Open Access Conference. Retrieved from www.berlin9.org/about/declaration.

Chan, Seb (2019). Fire, fire, fire: Words from creative state 2019. *Medium*. Retrieved from https://blog.usejournal.com/fire-fire-fire-words-from-creative-state-2019-b314f33da1c4.

Christen, Kimberly (2012). Does information really want to be free? Indigenous knowledge systems and the question of openness. *International Journal of Communication*, 6: 2870–93.

Duncan, Carol (1991). Art museums and the ritual of citizenship. In Steven D. Lavine (ed), *Exhibiting Cultures: The Poetics and Politics of Museum Display*. Washington, DC: Smithsonian Institution Press, pp. 88–103.

Flickr (2019). The commons. *Flickr*. Retrieved from www.flickr.com/commons/usage.

Habermas, Jürgen (1989 [1962]). *The Structural Transformation of the Public Sphere*. Trans. Thomas Burger and Frederick Lawrence. Cambridge, MA: MIT Press.

International Council of Museums (ICOM) 2019. Museum definition. Retrieved from https://icom.museum/en/resources/standards-guidelines/museum-definition.

Jafari, Aliakbar, Taheri, Babak and vom Lehn, Dirk (2013). Cultural consumption, interactive sociality, and the museum. *Journal of Marketing Management*, 29: 1729–52.

Kinsella, Eileen (2019). More than 75 New York galleries are slammed with lawsuits for allegedly violating the Americans with Disabilities Act. *Art Net News*, 29 January. Retrieved from https://news.artnet.com/art-world/dozens-of-new-york-galleries-slammed-with-lawsuits-for-ada-compliance-on-websites-1450276.

Mahey, M., Al-Abdulla, A., Ames, S. . . . Papaioannou, G. (2019). Open a GLAM lab. Digital cultural heritage innovation labs. Retrieved from https://glamlabs.pubpub.org.

The Met (2017). Introducing open access at the met. Retrieved from www.metmuseum.org/blogs/digital-underground/2017/open-access-at-the-met.

Microsoft (2020). Open access is transforming the way the public explores art. *Microsoft in Culture*. Retrieved from www.microsoft.com/inculture/arts/cleveland-museum-of-art-open-access.

Museums Association (2002). *Code of Ethics for Museums*. London: Museums Association. Retrieved from www.wipo.int/export/sites/www/tk/en/databases/creative_heritage/docs/museum_assn_code.pdf.

NeuroDigital Technologies (2020). Touching masterpieces. Retrieved from https://touchingmasterpieces.com.

Open Glam (2019). Why. Retrieved from https://openglam.org/why.

Ritzer, George and Jurgenson, Nathan (2010). Production, consumption, prosumption. *Journal of Consumer Culture*, 10(1): 13–36.

Sandell, Richard (1998). Museums as agents of social inclusion. *Museum Management and Curatorship*, 17(4): 401–418.

Scott, Carol (2010). Museums, the public and public value. *The Journal of Museum Education*, 35(1): 33–42.

Segal, Nina (2013). Masterworks for one and all. *The New York Times*, 29 May. Retrieved from www.nytimes.com/2013/05/29/arts/design/museums-mull-public-use-of-online-art-images.html.

Sherratt, Tim (2019). Hacking heritage: Understanding the limits of access. In Hannah Lewi, Wally Smith, Dirk vom Lehn and Steven Cooke (eds), *The Routledge International Handbook of New Digital Practices in Galleries, Libraries, Archives, Museums and Heritage Sites*. London: Routledge, pp. 116–30.

Singh, Supriya and Meredith, Blake (2012). The digitization of Pacific cultural collections: Consulting with Pacific diasporic communities and museum experts. *Curator: The Museum Journal*, 55(1): 95–105.

Springwise (2018). Innovations that matter. Retrieved from www.springwise.com/haptic-vr-gloves-allow-blind-experience-art.

Vergo, Peter (1989). *The New Museology*. London: Reaktion Books.

Weil, Stephen E. (2002). *Making Museums Matter*. New York: Smithsonian Press.

Wiedemann, Julia, Patzschke, Eva and Schmitt, Susanne (2019). Museums' strategies for opening up to open access: German museums' utilization logics for digital content. *Museum and Society*, 17: 193–209.

Winesmith, Keir and Carey, Anna (2014). Why build an API for a museum collection? San Francisco Museum of Modern Art. Retrieved from www.sfmoma.org/read/why-build-api-museum-collection.

3 From sensory to sensing museum

Introduction

This chapter uses the Museum of Old and New Art (MONA) in Hobart, Australia, as a case study, due to its early adoption of personalisation technology. It also draws on a wider engagement with materials drawn from interviews with cultural professionals and industry trade press to develop a larger account of sensory museums. The discussion canvasses the shifting sensory experience of the museum and explores the collapsing of digital media infrastructures with the historical sense-making practice of museum visitors. Sensors are explored as a particular facet of the process of platformisation that is the key to the online and on-site museum experience. The chapter focuses on the physical experience of the museum to argue that interactions that now take place in relation to smartphones and other forms of information collection, storage and analysis are altering how audiences experience collections. In turn, institutions and their exhibitions are reconfigured to enable new forms of always-on data capture.

The term 'sensor society' is used as an orienting concept by Andrejevic and Burdon (2015) to signify the growing embrace of systems that capture, store and use data. Its application to the sensory museum in this chapter is characterised by audiences using smartphones working in tandem with sensory architectures that provide visitors with varying forms of personalisation. This conceptualisation highlights the shifting boundaries of the museum as it flows through forms of digital mediation that may or may not be facilitated by the institution.

The museum has long been a sensory infrastructure. Touch and kiss were principal ways of accessing the mystic properties of relics by pilgrims in the sixteenth century (Classen 2017: 11). This custom was maintained in the seventeenth and eighteenth centuries, when museums such as the Ashmolean would invite visitors to chew objects and to manually handle artefacts (Classen 2017; Howes 2005). Museums endeavoured to stimulate the

DOI: 10.4324/9780429298691-3

physical senses of audiences in order to extend and share learning pedagogies. In this way, a range of multisensory experiences were drawn upon by the museum to promote multiple avenues of audience participation. It was felt that whole-body and sensory experiences would make objects and artworks accessible. Accordingly, the delivery of sensory access involved the museum managing physical stimulants to touch and smell as a resource that inspired wonder and learning in audiences.

Particular modalities of viewing have historically called upon the correct and structured ways of engaging with an exhibit. Guard rails guided visitor movement and wall labels included information from the curator about the work that formed the basis for correct interpretation. Wayfinding was also used to direct visitor attention to specific content and shape engagement (Mandel 2018). As the director of the Centre for Museology, University of Manchester, United Kingdom and former museum curator Helen Rees Leahy (2012: 4) points out, 'The material, social and institutional experience of navigating museum artifacts has continually been recalibrated in accordance with changing practices of display and visuality'. Museum spectators participated in a series of actions that affirmed their understanding of the exhibit and cultural competency. Usually this involved the museum providing specific guidance about how to behave with regard to touching objects and in terms of the level of restraint required. Examples include guidebooks and periodicals provided to women and the working class that demonstrated various modes of mindful observation, which they were encouraged to replicate. Signage was used to encourage visitors to experience artworks through 'sight alone' (Classen 2017: 9). Through these modes of participation, the institution conceived the audiences' cultural competency and, as a result, their ability to correctly interpret the exhibition (Rees Leahy 2012).

In the era of sensory devices, the museum is routinely transmitted to audiences through digital means. Almost anyone has access to culture so long as they own a device and are prepared to use it, or in some cases have access to a VPN service to avoid sanctions on search engines and artworks deemed to be too provocative. Sometimes this involves visitors taking pictures of artefacts that they post to social media or searching online open access collections. As Giannini and Bowen (2019) point out, one correct narrative becomes problematic for museums whose visitors are finding themselves gaining improved knowledge using digital tools. There is less demand for the contemporary museum to maintain an authoritative voice as audiences have grown accustomed to seeking out answers to questions on the internet and asking voice-controlled intelligent assistants, such as Siri and Alexa, for information.

You might say that the digital layer is bridging the spatial temporal and social experience of the museum. This involves and requires a seamless transition of the physicality of the institution towards automated processes that organise interactions and make connections that might not otherwise be possible. While attention has already been paid to the sensorisation of the museum and artworks (Classen 2017; Howes et al. 2018; Parry and Sawyer 2005), these accounts don't necessarily discuss how specific institutions are integrating digital technologies into the audience experience or which technologies the audience adopts easily with attributable benefits. Owing to the ease of information access enabled as a result of the practices of media platforms including Google and Facebook, a rebalancing has occurred between institutions and their audiences.

It is possible that static labels and traditional forms of wayfinding can be challenging for contemporary visitors who are accustomed to using their smartphones to access a range of perspectives immediately online. In other words, it matters that museums haven't typically provided multiple forms of interpretation and digital devices, and platforms can potentially solve this problem. The previous chapter argued that digital platforms and media devices help to enhance access but can also blur the imperatives of the museum. Here the significance of museums adopting sensory architectures and the implications of them continuing to occupy a participatory and transparent role for the collection, preservation, research, interpretation and exhibition of artefacts are canvassed. There is a penetration of platform infrastructures, logics and frameworks into the museum (Gillespie 2018) that increases the risk of the visitor becoming a source of information to be deconstructed and datafied. Unlike platforms that monetise their processing capacities, the museum is mostly drawing on data-collection practices to improve efficiency and effectiveness. Foot traffic heat maps, for example, are used by some institutions to generate data about audience flows and common visitor paths and can be used to ensure that the exhibition achieves its goals (Strohaier et al. 2015).

MONA case study of the 'O'

MONA in Tasmania, Australia, has integrated the use of public handheld devices, which it supplies to each visitor upon arrival; it is therefore referenceable as an example of a sensory museum. Located on a remote island at the southernmost tip of Australia, MONA opened on 22 January 2011 to critical acclaim in the art world internationally, largely due to its disruptive use of participatory technology. It was the sole vision of David Walsh, a millionaire collector who made his fortune by developing a sports gambling system. The $200 million museum combines its art and artefacts with bars and lounge areas, a small vineyard, microbrewery and boutique hotel and is the site of a proposed casino. MONA is by its very design an 'anti-museum'

From sensory to sensing museum 41

(Franklin 2020). Set in its picturesque winery, the striking museum appears as an underground bunker with no windows, cut into the Triassic sandstone of the bank of the Derwent River. Covering almost 10,000 m² of exhibition space over three levels, it feels a little like a nightclub. To make visiting MONA additionally intriguing, you board a high-speed catamaran for a 25-minute journey up the river from the city (see Figure 3.1).

In opposition to an elitist institution that instructs audiences on how to experience objects, MONA unapologetically seeks to break with convention and distances itself from the philosophies that underpin past modes of visitation. With no clear entrance, visitors follow the trail of people to the largely subterranean building and, after climbing 99 steps, they are greeted by synthetic tennis courts and an unmarked mirrored doorway. After paying the entrance fee, one descends a spiral staircase 17 m underground to a basement cordoned by an imposing 250-million-year-old Triassic sandstone wall. Visitors are met by attendants who offer them an 'O', a museum-owned mobile device, or the option to download the app onto their own smartphone (see Figure 3.2).

Provided with onscreen instructions on how to operate the handheld device, the visitor is then left to discover the museum on their own. Without a set path to follow or clear signage, the visitor must make decisions about where to go and what to view. Replacing traditional wall labels, the 'O' pushes content through a Radio Frequency Identification (RFID) tag that works in conjunction with wireless sensors located in the ceiling of the institution. Also available as an app, the 'O' identifies user location and proximity to artefacts and compiles a list of relevant works nearby. Guests go about navigating the space on their own terms, controlling the information they receive about objects as they move through the museum spaces, their direction to the next artefact provided by the 'O' potentially at the expense of missing entire sections of the gallery.

The 'O' provides opportunities for people to rate artworks by loving or hating them and displays on the screen how many others agree with their

Figure 3.1 James Turrell's Amarna at MONA, 2015.

Source: Image by Michael Fromholtz is licensed under CC BY-SA 4.0. https://creativecommons.org/licenses/by/2.0/?ref=ccsearch&atype=rich

Figure 3.2 The 'O' pod at MONA.

Source: Image by Rob Taylor from London, UK is licensed under CC BY 2.0. https://creativecommons.org/licenses/by-sa/4.0/deed.en

appraisal. The audio on the media device itself is entertaining. Visitors can elect to listen to audio descriptions with explanations voiced by artists and academics in formal curatorial style or by David Walsh himself. The 'save visit' function on the guide/app also makes it possible to view the institution and revisit information about particular works afterwards – it is essentially a playback feature for your visit.

What is especially significant about MONA's use of the 'O' is that it signalled the broadening adoption of smartphones, tablets and other devices into the interpretation of museum exhibits along with the superimposing of digital layers of engagement into cultural experiences. At the time of its release in 2011, cultural workers who were interviewed for this book expressed a desire to use a similar navigation system reinforcing MONA's significance as a future-focused institution. Part of the appeal of the 'O' was that it appeared less elitist and seemed to overcome some of the access issues experienced by audiences to other galleries and museums, because it served to reduce the function of attendants to interpret artefacts and extended the on-site experience of the museum online. Unsurprisingly, other institutions soon followed suit, releasing similar navigation systems that exploited smartphone technology and aimed to create a feedback loop between the audience and institution. Gallery spaces are increasingly saturated with augmented reality (AR), VR and AI to provide audiences with an enhanced institutional narrative and speak to the identity of the museum as envisioning a more interactive and participatory relationship with its visitors.

In this vein, the Cooper Hewitt, when it reopened after a long renovation, released a sensor in a pen. This interactive stylus worked in conjunction with wall labels with a near-field communication (NFC) tag – essentially, small microchips able to send identification information that can be read by smart devices when scanned. Industry leader Seb Chan and Lucie Paterson, Head of Experience Product and Digital at the Australian Centre for the Moving Image in Melbourne, credit the Cooper Hewitt pen and Apple's use of NFC 'reading capabilities in iOS 12' as influential in 'exhibit design companies and museums re-examining how technology of that nature might contribute to a "smart museum"' (Museums and the Web and Paterson 2019). Touching artefacts with the pen, visitors at the Cooper Hewitt access enriched information about objects, which can be collected and viewed online afterwards. While described at its release as the 'holy grail in museum circles', it was withdrawn from the museum floor during the pandemic as a result of concerns that it could spread COVID-19 (Straup Cope 2020). Similarly, the Hirshhorn Museum in Washington launched 'Hi' in 2018, a mobile museum guide that draws on image recognition so that visitors can scan artefacts in order to listen to the information voiced by artists, curators, scientists and historians (Smithsonian 2018). Like the 'O', it provides real-time information about viewed objects and delivers a retrospective timeline of visits via email. However, unlike the 'O', 'Hi' includes video content and increased accessibility features such as voiceover for onscreen text and captions for audio and video content, as well as an interactive map.

MONA as a sensory museum

MONA's adoption of new strategies in information storage, collection and analysis makes it a fitting example and suitable case study of a sensory museum, due to its articulation of technologies, resources, labour and relationships with the tech industry. The purpose-built site comprises an infrastructure consisting of a material media system made up of data connectivity, compute power, proximity sensors and software; these are integrated to oversee visitor movement throughout the building and respond in real time. The media/data infrastructure alters the museum's social practices. Engagement with the exhibition takes place aided and formatted by the device and is mediated by algorithms, databases and networks of distributed storage.

While it would be an overstatement to suggest that the device enables a democratisation of the museum, it is important to recognise that as the audiences navigate MONA, they develop confidence. The media device protects the audience from experiencing a certain level of discomfort and confusion in the process, establishing a different pattern of viewing artefacts. Trudi Brinckman, a curator at MONA, describes the 'O' on the website of Art Processors, the company that designed the device:

> [It is] a powerful medium that connects the artwork and the viewer [which] . . . brings three things together: the life of the person, the technology, and the artwork, creating an incredible experience that is completely individual, and far more fulfilling than just showing them a wall label with information.
>
> (Art Processors 2018)

In a way, the media device stands in for traditional forms of wayfinding or other forms of instruction, which direct visitor attention to specific content (Mandel 2018). There is a transformation of the visual and aural display functions of the institution. Despite the fact that attendants are located throughout MONA, the media device significantly reduces additional layers of interpretation, information or guidance that they would normally provide. The path a visitor travels is dynamically guided by the media device's suggestions, which take the visitor to exhibits of their choice. The audience interacts and exerts power by making specific choices about what they will and won't see and the order in which they will view artefacts. By voting about whether they like specific objects, it becomes possible to express taste preferences and get immediate feedback about how this opinion resonates with other visitors.

In this way, the 'O' addresses a perceived structural imbalance between the museum and audience by creating a format where visitors can gain a sense they are contributing to the overarching exhibition and their experience. A shared experience emerges as visitors go about the process of using it to interact with artworks. The device is the key to how viewers interpret the artworks and recall them afterwards, narrating back to them the order in which they toured the museum. Through their interactions, the visitor curates their own on-site experience simply through their movements, potentially missing objects and whole areas of the museum but with a sense that they experienced the highlights in an independent and personalised way.

Undeniably, the 'O' creates a format where the audience makes meaning within what would appear to be an open-ended cultural encounter. When once on the receiving end of a one-way stream of information, the 'O' overcomes a range of challenges that audiences can experience when navigating artefacts. This sensorisation of the museum environment constitutes a major shift in how culture has been curated and received by museum visitors over the past few decades and marks a new sensibility that is characterised by new forms of 'always-on' data collection. One might say that the museum purposely responds to normative modes of cultural exclusion by embedding user participation into its digital architecture. This has shifted how audiences participate in the production of cultural experiences (Hawker and Carah 2020).

At MONA, the museum visitor acts as a 'probe' whose movement enables monitoring and tracking within a device-space ecosystem where data are collected as they roam the institution (Andrejevic and Burdon 2015: 206). Location feedback software (proximity location) that draws on the visitors' use of media devices is imbedded within the development of the museum's information architecture for the purpose of collecting behavioural data and optimising the viewing experience. Visitors engage with artefacts and move around a ubiquitous environment, which collects data as they go about engaging with the artefacts. When a visitor dwells upon a particular object, or moves through the exhibition, the museum is informed in real time. In this way, the data-collection practices that are enacted by social media platforms relating to user participation are adopted by MONA to create new opportunities for interaction. The visitor proximity system makes apparent which artworks visitors engage with and the routes that they take as they navigate the museum.

The 'O' becomes intricately interconnected with the on-site experience of the museum, bringing together the physical with the virtual while also informing the institution's decision-making about popular artefacts, paths travelled by visitors and how engaging the device's translations, factual backgrounds and consumable data are. The institution listens and responds uniquely to the user in real time as they move through the exhibition, closing the loop between the human feedback and the machine dialogue. The 'O' is a mediator that improves the overall quality of the audience visit, which is enhanced as a result of the museum's capacity to draw on data to calculate and engineer a new kind of experience.

The museum as a sensory infrastructure

The 'O' is one articulation of a sensory museum that shares similar attributes with other visitor companions that draw on advanced technology. The following interviews and discussions with cultural workers and an analysis of industry documents develop an account of how these institutions and exhibits are produced. The aim is to pay attention to the process by which cultural professionals, who are not necessarily technology experts, individually negotiate the adoption or expansion of their interactive and participatory culture. Despite cultural workers describing forms of interactivity in different ways, from beacons used to push content through to AR-based apps designed to engage audiences, they routinely acknowledged the importance of layering it into on-site cultural engagements.

One Australian-based cultural director explained that more people are 'accessing information or creating it in a digital environment – that's the place where we belong'. In a talk addressing culture industry experts at Museum Next, IBM business strategy leader for libraries and museums at Microsoft Catherine Devine suggests that by incorporating a 'digital layer', the museum can better consider its exhibitional practices in relation to audience needs in order to make decisions (Museum Next 2019). She describes this as allowing institutions to select the 'right language, for the right person at the right time' (Museum Next 2019). With this ideology, technologies are imagined as interwoven with the built form of the museum. Aggregate datasets are embraced as enabling rich cultural experiences that hold the potential to boost visitor satisfaction (Museum Next 2019).

The algorithms governing this interaction take note of users' location and their interest in a particular artefact, and push to them targeted, engaging content, obscuring less desirable objects. Flexibility and adaptability are central to a prototype of an institution that is less rigid and able to be immediately responsive to its audience. The architecture of the museum changes in real time based upon audience interests as a dynamic feedback loop.

While museum workers acknowledge that digital platforms won't necessarily replace the real, they have become a central part of the museum experience. The museum and its exhibitions are imagined as rich in media content, shifting focus from on-site exhibitions in some cases to 'digital first' (Hartig 2018). Chief experience officer at the Australian Centre for the Moving Image in Melbourne, Seb Chan, uses the term the 'magic circle' on his blog; he ports this from game studies to explain that visitors should experience superpowers within the museum (Chan 2019). While not the sole provider of visitor superpowers, he says technology can help to make the museum 'more accessible, persistent or unique' and can assist visitors in gaining a 'contextual understanding of works and objects, or just a comfort in being challenged by new ideas'. Importantly, he highlights the need for interactivity 'built-in and designed from the start' (Chan 2019). On the whole, museum workers are embracing change that enhances visitor experience and their institution's ability to be effective and desirable. Some interviewees challenged the idea that museums should adapt digital layers to better engage the audience. One Australian director argued against embracing new forms of interactivity and instead suggested that museums had 'real things [the artefacts] and shouldn't try to compete with the virtual world of game designers'. This perspective stood in stark contrast to the way other informants imagined integrating technology and how they discussed working to bring it into being within the museum. These institutions, in the words of a New Zealand-based curator, 'are trying to add more and more layers, into the onsite visitor's experience'.

Predicting what the future museum will be like helps cultural workers characterise new ways of working and ways in which cultural institutions might incorporate technology. Another director of an Australian museum discussed the imperative to build digital into the museum 'at the start' so that it 'just is'. What seems particularly difficult for the interviewees to imagine is visitor agency being realised outside of a technological ecosystem – for example, audiences are depicted as scanning, swiping and navigating the museum using phones. As head of collections and cultural environments at Västernorrlands Museum, Kajsa Hartig (2018), explains in a blog on Medium: 'Building capacity for a digital first museum experience, that delivers value, means as a first step, understanding the audience's behaviors online and where they could possibly encounter the museum'. There is an assumption, in her opinion, that visitors will want to navigate the museum in the same way that they browse the internet. Shifts in how people access content on the internet are often cited by cultural workers as making it necessary for the museum to become a more responsive environment. The physical experience of the institution is regarded as needing to straddle the digital.

One US-based museum consultant expands upon this idea, describing the dynamic relationship among visitors, exhibitions and handheld devices:

> The biggest two potential changes for museums are knowledge sharing and the blurring of the distinction between the accredited expert and the anybody – the enthusiast, the eyewitness. . . . If you look at the way that Amazon works [books at Amazon], I put in a word that I am interested in and they give me everything I want in the main picture. On the side they give me people's views/reviews of it and if it is a good product. Citizen input – if people have read this book you should read that other book. You have a new friend and you can decide.

Online shopping was drawn upon as an example by one museum consultant, to depict how the contemporary museum should operate. There is a presumption that the distance between the museum, the facilitator and the audience is closed through the embedding of a digital system on-site. Ratings, comments and other feedback loops make it possible for the museum to gain an informed insight into audience expectations and identify future improvements. Importantly, the sensory institution facilitates opportunities for visitors to engage with objects on their own terms rather than through the provision of one set curatorial narrative (Wilson-Barnao 2018). A similar approach is found on online websites, including Amazon and Netflix, where there are levers for personalisation and rating systems that give consumers the ability to express their opinion via a click. In this way, this museum consultant imagines museums replicating core forms of data collection for the purposes of engagement and curated experience.

An Australian museum interviewee reinforced the necessity to recalibrate museum exhibition practices:

> We have to be aware that everyone has information in their pocket – we are no longer the gatekeepers but the piquers of interest. We can't hold all the information because everyone has the internet and a smartphone. Everyone has more information in their pocket than you are putting into the exhibition. Instead, we [as a museum] are thinking about what kind of experiences can we create that are unique?

This museum worker described it as a given that audiences will engage with exhibits using a smartphone and furthers the idea that education is a journey and the presentation of an artefact can be the start of visitor interest, with the task of the museum being to present channels for further exploration and understanding, using the tools with which the visitor is most familiar.

By being woven into the physicality of a museum, handheld devices are central to the ways cultural audiences access information and can be regarded as offering a less hierarchical context for learning. The institution and its artworks act as a starting point for different forms of digital interactivity and participation (see Figure 3.3). The same interviewee discussed the importance of the museum adopting a 'User Experience' (UX) mindset, an approach that is used to manage how users interface interactive systems, such as websites, or web or desktop applications, when incorporating technology on-site:

> They [online interfaces] get the benefit that you can't go to the next screen until you have pressed the right buttons or read a particular message. We [museums] don't get that benefit . . . we have to work in the way that they do but with wayfinding, games or software in the space.

This interviewee recognised the need for exhibits to become attuned to how visitors interact with objects and described an increasingly intelligent museum. There is recognition that visitors use smartphones before they visit and while they are on-site, and again use them afterwards to view objects online. The kinds of enabling conditions articulated by cultural

From sensory to sensing museum 49

Figure 3.3 Signage at exhibitions encourages visitors to document and share their experiences on social media using hashtags and posting. This image depicts a sign at the APT9 exhibition at QGoMA, Brisbane, Australia.

Source: This image was taken at the Queensland Gallery of Modern Art (QGoMA).

professionals involve sensing the movements of visitors as they move through a museum that responds in real time. Similar to what Angelo Chianese and Francesco Piccialli (2015) describe as a smart museum, interactive objects work in tandem with audiences within an Internet of Things (IoT) architecture. Chianese and Piccialli (2015) acknowledge that the IoT connection of interactive devices is a complex puzzle, but as we are able to add light and pressure sensitivity to artefacts, connection, interactivity and experience will be enhanced. Much of what they articulate is about striving to keep pace with widespread shifts that will allow the museum to straddle its accessibility, education, visitor experience, engagement and online concerns.

This is especially notable in the digital strategies of cultural institutions. The Andy Warhol Museum in Pittsburgh, for example, makes its digital strategy available on GitHub, a web-based code hosting interface, where the organisation describes its on-site approach in this way:

> With respect to digital technologies, the on-site experience must not be intrusive or overbearing. Digital initiatives must be easily available when visitors want them and invisible when they don't. The digital components must align with visitor behavior patterns and augment the analog museum experience in tasteful, meaningful and interesting ways.
>
> (Warhol Museum 2016)

Interaction takes place through connected devices and sensitive artefacts, in conjunction with a sensory architecture.

A key part of the decision-making around exhibition design hinges on delving deeper into the components of an exhibition and gaining a stronger understanding of the audience experience. When describing on-site gallery experience, the *Tate Digital Strategy 2013–2015: Digital as a Dimension of Everything* states:

> Digital technologies will transform visitors' experiences in the galleries. Wi-Fi will be enabled in all galleries, and extensions to the mobile website, designed for in-gallery use, will allow access to a wealth of information and interpretation about the works on view in the museum. Information staff will be able to access and share information with visitors using tablet computers.
>
> (Stack 2013)

The arrangement of Wi-Fi, interactives and navigation systems is regarded as promoting audience understanding. It becomes possible for the museum to respond to audience curiosity by pushing forms of media-rich content, or by making changes in response to new data as they arise. You might say that there is a transformation of the museum into a ubiquitous environment for the benefit of 'any person'.

An advisor to the Australian museum sector describes a museum that is

> underpinned by new forms of interactivity. I can picture a gallery full of technology and sensors and screens . . . it might link to public communication . . . that allows people to explore the data. Or it might be a

facade that displays in real time what the water consumption is inside the building for instance.

New forms of interactivity are taking place that are often regarded as a more powerful way to deliver information to visitors that was not previously available.

Cultural workers often articulate concerns about the commercial data practices of social media platforms, but the explanations of this phenomenon can normalise a double standard whereby the museum is regarded as needing to better manage data while somehow sitting outside the same set of ethical concerns. A respected strategic planning consultant to the Australian cultural sector explained how museums could look to the practices of media platforms in this way:

> [Social media] gives information [to people] that they want to hear at the point at which they want to hear it . . . they have a pretty good profile of exactly what your interest points are. I think there are lessons for museums which are: understanding audiences and what they care about.

Museum professionals see apps and guides as a means to collect metrics, which increases overall satisfaction. There is a clear desire to accurately personalise visitor experiences and to use algorithms and databases to develop additional layers of content, which can be added to artworks accessed through a media device. While the real artworks invite visitor contemplation, the smartphone is used in conjunction with its algorithmic systems and apps to unlock hidden narratives that provide detailed context around the artist and the artwork.

In August 2019, the Tate Modern in the United Kingdom opened its virtual wing where it housed an AR experience to engage audiences with selected artworks. For two years, the gallery worked with Spark AR, Mill Interactive and Facebook Creative Shop to develop a series of artworks where audiences use the Instagram camera on their phone to scan a name tag, which directs them towards eight artworks with AR capacity. Viewing these works through the lens of Instagram, it is possible to experience different AR effects, including animated scenes, 3D rendering and overlays, to show the untold stories of the selected artworks. Matthew Roberts, product manager from Spark AR, explicitly described this important form of algorithmic engagement and its role in interpreting artworks on the Tech@ facebook website:

> Today's smartphones have both immense computing power and an always-on connection to the internet. More than just capture, this is a

camera that can see. By tapping into a wealth of relevant data alongside AI and computer vision algorithms, we can help people learn and connect to the world around them in meaningful ways. (Tech@facebook 2019)

Roberts described the benefits of the integration of the media platform into the museum and its capacity to shape cultural experiences. The novel and immersive use of the artworks within the Tate virtual wing are specifically designed to appeal to audiences accustomed to participatory and open-ended forms of engagement. The media platform works to translate the artworks into a format that is credited as enhancing the cultural experience because it allows the visitor to better decipher and understand it. As most interviewees' reflections demonstrate, there is a desire for architectures that are purposefully designed as automated spaces. The smartphone becomes integral to a mode of viewing that creatively appropriates artworks and seeks out new forms of audience interaction and data.

This perspective of anticipating and thinking about the visitor is resulting in museums partnering with technology companies and establishing incubators that aim to encourage new ideas and approaches. In 2020, the Contemporary Art Museum in Wroclaw, Poland, a branch of the National Museum, partnered with IBM to use the AI of its Watson app to engage visitors at the *Paradise* at the *Willmann Opus Magnum* exhibit (Szymuk 2020). Utilising a provided smartphone and headset, visitors were able to use the AI of the Watson app to ask questions about the paintings and receive real-time feedback in Polish. Each visitor interaction in turn worked to continue to train the machine learning model, better enabling it to respond to future questions. The museum's utilisation of the IBM Watson AI demonstrates that the audience is conceived as active participants who engage with media content and become visible within a sensory infrastructure. While depictions of museums in the press and popular culture focus on their need to become participatory mostly for economic reasons, there is an argument that an important and complicated logic is at play. Specifically, museums' efforts to become more participatory are part of an accommodation to, and adoption of, the logics of a digital media infrastructure characterised by both publicity and monitoring. In this media infrastructure, the visibility of different publics is crucial to the publicity efforts of the museum. Generating publicity for a museum both advances the public value of the institution and simultaneously integrates the museum into the wider market logic of the digital economy.

The digital director of the National Gallery, London, reinforced this concept in a recent talk at 'Museum Next', where he argued that 'museums need to think differently if they are to become better structured for risk' (Museum Next and Michaels 2018). He suggested that museums have evolved from a decades-old operating model oriented around the achievement of social justice that makes it incompatible with the digital economy. Michaels theorised that in order for the museum to better mitigate risks, it is required to 'flip that idea around' and better explore its new position in the economy. This will help the museum to 'stop being so fragile' (Museum Next 2018). He referenced the National Gallery and the ACMI among others as examples of Innovation Labs that align themselves with the creative industries and the digital, corporate, academic and government sectors. By seeking out public–private partnerships, in his view, the museum is able to create an environment where it can test out different ideas and commercial models.

Conclusion

The cultural workers' views canvassed in this chapter echo and uphold the benefits of platformisation to the museum: enhanced personalisation, the layering of multiple narratives, the need for better data management and on-demand content. There is a desire to seek out alternative business models and partnerships that extend beyond the museum's usual way of operating and engaging. The examples in this chapter demonstrate profound shifts in the digital architecture of cultural institutions, from Innovation Labs housed within the museum itself to the establishing of exhibition-specific digital infrastructures. Without question, smartphones and other similar personalised media devices are being used as tools of perception and navigation by contemporary museum visitors.

Cultural workers appear to articulate and understand the risks associated with the practices of social media platforms, but these concerns are minimised by dialogue that situates the museum as separate or outside of these practices. These processes and practices are not always instigated or controlled by the museum. There is a wider belief that digital devices are synonymous with audience empowerment (Black 2005; Bourriaud 2002; Simon 2010) and an opening of the museum to the public. Digital platforms appear to be regarded as extending the on-site experience online, working to stand in for the physical institution by enhancing its visitor education, community-building exhibitionary practices and publicity. There is an acknowledgement that the digital economy creates benefits and efficiencies that the museum must embrace, or risk exclusion and obscurity from the public eye and financial insecurity.

The sensory museum is an aspirational space in the sense that it exists both as an idea in the mind of cultural workers and as a reality insofar as it is starting to happen within the museum. It is characterised as a museum that is more agile and dynamic. It occupies a space that operates as a medium for supplying unlimited content within a ubiquitous infrastructure. It yields a disruption of the museum's traditional model and an alignment with visitors, who are encouraged to roam freely using smartphones 'that are synchronised with' labels, artworks and 'personalisation strategies' (Wilson-Barnao 2018: 104). The museum acts as a 'learning archive that stimulates user engagement', in turn responding to 'individual tastes and interests' (Wilson-Barnao 2018: 104). The museum aids audience engagement by creating new levers for visitors to exert their influence and interact with the museum. Information is collected by the museum for the purpose of revealing hidden insights into audience behaviour and generating new ways to present exhibitions and objects. Artworks are understood as open-ended experiences that facilitate a process that enables the audience to get real-time responses from the institution.

There is a diminishing desire for a single curatorial narrative and a remodelling of the museum from a space that is underwritten by traditional forms of research to one geared towards developing the institution as a media infrastructure that is able to make real-time judgements about the user experience (Carah and Angus 2018). The museum audience performs the work of producing data as people experience exhibits, which in turn enables the museum to respond. This shift allows museums to gain a holistic look at data across different departments and use it in combination.

The next chapter turns to the collapsing of the boundaries of the museum with digital platforms and algorithmic media to explore different models of collaboration.

References

Andrejevic, Mark and Burdon, Mark (2015). Defining the sensor society. *Television & New Media*, 16(1): 19–36.
Art Processors (2018). Not just for kids: How art processors is helping MONA drive engagement with family-friendly content. Retrieved from www.artprocessors. net/articles/not-just-kids-how-art-processors-helping-mona-drive-engagement-family-friendly-content.
Black, Graham (2005). *The Engaging Museum: Developing Museums for Visitor Involvement*. New York: Routledge.
Bourriaud, Nicolas (2002). *Esthétique relationelle (Relational Aesthetics)*. Dijon: Les Presses du Réel.
Carah, Nicholas and Angus, Daniel (2018). Algorithmic brand culture: Participatory labour, machine learning and branding on social media. *Media, Culture & Society*, 40(2): 178–94.
Chan, Seb (2019). On immersion & interactivity via #MW2019. *Medium*. Retrieved from https://sebchan.medium.com/on-immersion-interactivity-via-mw2019-ac72d9c700bd.

Chianese, Angelo and Piccialli, Francesco (2015). SmaCH: A framework for smart cultural heritage spaces. Proceedings of the 10th International Conference on Signal-Image Technology and Internet-Based Systems, pp. 477–84. Retrieved from www.researchgate.net/publication/282886980_SmaCH_A_Framework_for_Smart_Cultural_Heritage_Spaces.

Classen, Constance (2017). *The Museum of the Senses Experiencing Art and Collections*. London: Bloomsbury.

Franklin, Adrian (2020). *Anti-museum*. London: Routledge.

Giannini, Tula and Bowen, Jonathan P. (2019). Museums and digitalism. In *Museums and Digital Culture: New Perspectives and Research*. New York: Springer, pp. 27–46.

Gillespie, Tarleton (2018). *Custodians of the Internet: Platforms, Content Moderation, and the Hidden Decisions that Shape Social Media*. New Haven, CT: Yale University Press.

Hartig, Kajsa (2018). The museum experience as digital first: Strategic approaches to content, conversation and audience engagement. *Medium*. Retrieved from https://medium.com/@kajsahartig/the-museum-experience-as-digital-first-strategic-approaches-to-content-conversation-and-audience-ada4b3fbc6bf.

Hawker, Kiah and Carah, Nicholas (2020). Snapchat's augmented reality brand culture: Sponsored filters and lenses as digital piecework. *Continuum*. doi:10.1080/10304312.2020.1827370.

Howes, David (2005). *Empire of the Senses: The Sensual Culture Reader*. Oxford: Berg.

Howes, David, Clarke, Eric, Macpherson, Fiona, Best, Beverley and Cox, Rupert (2018). Sensing art and artifacts: Explorations in sensory museology. *The Senses and Society*, 13(3): 317–34.

Mandel, Lauren H. (2018). Understanding and describing users' wayfinding behavior in public library facilities. *Journal of Librarianship and Information Science*, 50(1): 23–33.

Museum Next (2018). Film: New strategic thinking for museums. Retrieved from www.museumnext.com/article/new-strategic-thinking-for-museums.

Museum Next (2019). The 'digital layer' in museums. *Vimeo*. Retrieved from https://vimeo.com/340763046.

Museum Next and Michaels, Chris (2018). Film: New strategic thinking for museums. Retrieved from www.museumnext.com/article/new-strategic-thinking-for-museums.

Museums and the Web and Paterson, Lucie (2019). End-to-end experience design: Lessons for all from the NFC-enhanced lost map of Wonderland. *MW19 Boston*. Retrieved from https://mw19.mwconf.org/paper/end-to-end-experience-design-lessons-for-all-from-the-nfc-enhanced-lost-map-of-wonderland%E2%80%8A-2.

Parry, Ross and Sawyer, Andrew (2005). Space and the machine: Adaptive museums, pervasive technology and the new gallery environment. In Suzanne Macleod (ed), *Reshaping Museum Space*. London: Routledge, pp. 39–53.

Rees Leahy, Helen (2012). *Museum Bodies: The Politics and Practices of Visiting and Viewing*. Aldershot: Ashgate.

Simon, Nina (2010). *The Participatory Museum*. Santa Cruz, CA: Creative Commons. Retrieved from www.participatorymuseum.org.

Smithsonian (2018). Hirshhorn launches new generation of museum mobile video guide. Retrieved from www.si.edu/newsdesk/releases/hirshhorn-launches-new-generation-museum-mobile-video-guide.

Stack, John (2013). *Tate Digital Strategy 2013–15: Digital as a Dimension of Everything*. London: Tate Gallery. Retrieved from www.tate.org.uk/research/publications/tate-papers/19/tate-digital-strategy-2013-15-digital-as-a-dimension-of-everything#:~:text=Tate%20Digital%20Strategy%202013%E2%80%9315%3A%20Digital%20as%20a%20Dimension%20of%20Everything,-John%20Stack&text=Throu.

Straup Cope, Aaron (2020). Bring your own pen device. *Aaronland*. Retrieved from www.aaronland.info/weblog/2020/06/16/revisiting.

Strohaier, Robert, Sprung, Gerhard, Nischelwitzer, Alexander and Schadenbauer, Sandra (2015). Using visitor-flow visualization to improve visitor experience in museums and exhibitions. *MW2015: Museums and the Web 2015*. Retrieved from https://mw2015.museumsandtheweb.com/paper/enhancing-visitor-experience-and-fostering-museum-popularity-through-deep-insights-in-the-placement-of-exhibits-by-new-techniques-in-visitor-flow-visualization-in-space-and-time.

Szymuk, Jaroslaw (2020). On the Baroque art trail with IBM Watson. Retrieved from www.ibm.com/blogs/southeast-europe/on-the-baroque-art-trail-with-ibm-watson.

Tech@facebook (2019). Augmenting abstraction: Facebook Expands AR Experiences with Tate. Retrieved from Augmenting abstraction: Facebook Expands AR Experiences with Tate (fb.com)

Warhol Museum (2016). Experiences and engagement: The Warhol Museum digital strategy. Retrieved from https://github.com/thewarholmuseum/digital-strategy/blob/master/02_Experiences_and_Engagement.md.

Wilson-Barnao, Caroline (2018). The logic of platforms: How 'on demand' museums are adapting in the digital era. *Critical Arts*, 32(3): 1–16.

4 From museum to platform

Introduction

The museum as an institution is constructed from a number of tangible components, which include objects, exhibitions, information, metadata and social connection, as well as some less tangible components, such as reputation and thought leadership through academic research. This chapter develops the argument that the temporal concern with access and integration of technology into these different tangible components lays the groundwork for the platformisation of the museum. Platforms appear to offer museums what they have been looking for, but there is a parallel intrusion of the economic and governmental infrastructures into its operations (Poell, Nieborg and van Dijck 2019). To begin, a history of mediatisation, the museum and the public sphere is presented. Contemporary examples of the platformised participation of cultural audiences, ranging from the use of chatbots at Anne Frank House in Amsterdam right through to online interfaces such as Google Arts and Culture (GAC), are provided with the aim of exploring the benefits and complications for the museum as an increasingly interconnected and networked public sphere.

The history of mediatisation, the museum and the public sphere

This brief historical consideration reviews the legacy relationship between museums, media and the public sphere, before taking into account the nature of platformisation. It is important to note that, due to its evolution from the collections of the church and royalty, the museum is widely contested as a public sphere. It wasn't until the Louvre Museum in Paris opened to the public in 1973 (Hooper-Greenhill 1992) and museum exhibitions appealed to the interests of a broader public that it assumed a role in the construction of an audience (Barrett 2011; Bennett 1995; Heumann Gurian

DOI: 10.4324/9780429298691-4

2006; McClellan 1994; Weil 2002). The early 2000s marked a period when the previous configurations of the museum passed into the archives of history and a new body of literature in museology argued for the museum to move towards a participatory and interactive configuration. Central to this ideology was the concept of 'museums as places of community activity, inclusion, well-being and belonging' (Bishop 2012; Black 2005; Bourriaud 2002; Simon 2010).

Following this period of redefinition, participation has become central to the way of working (Sandell 1998). Other researchers, including Graham Black (2005), refer to participation in terms of engagement. Across a number of institutional practices, there is a growing view and some consensus that participatory experiences advance the institution's educative capacity and public purpose. Museum professionals identified that the museum must change rapidly to stay current or popular, as well as economically viable, and tried to find new ways to engage visitors and establish relationships with audiences.

While the public sphere as initially conceived by Habermas (1989) – as one of all people participating as equals, regardless of their differences – has always been somewhat idealised, it does present a useful framework for considering the changing role of the museum as it develops new literacies, strategies and ways of working. Habermas's formation of the public sphere was similar to the Greek town square – a physical place where individuals came together to freely and rationally discuss and debate issues of mutual concern (Habermas 1989: 29), a place where status did not prevent participation in the conceptualisation of public opinion (Habermas 1989: 36, 43). For Habermas, the development of public opinion required having a public or body of citizens free from state sanctions and limitations with regard to class, gender, race and education, to be able to engage in public discussion about public affairs or issues affecting the society as a whole. Rather than force, rank or privilege determining the outcome of a decision, publicity provided the environment for better argument and consequently better collective decision-making (Habermas 1989: 208). In particular, 'critical publicity' plays a nascent role in the framework for a healthy public sphere. It has the capacity to restore the ideal speech situation by making vested market interests visible to different publics (Habermas 1989: 208). This form of publicity enables democracy because it enables anyone to announce 'personal inclinations, wishes and convictions – opinions' and realise them through 'rational-critical' public debate (Habermas 1989: 178, 219). 'Manipulative publicity' differs as it works to shape public opinion by distorting market interests (Habermas 1989: 200).

Like all culture industries, the museum relies on attracting visitors and attention. Everyday visitors to the museum gain a sense of participation as

From museum to platform 59

the photographs they share on social media of themselves 'doing' inside the museum (at least in part) demonstrates a flattening of the museum's once hierarchical and authoritative structure. This perspective is echoed in the comments of cultural workers and policy documents discussed in Chapter 2. Audiences talk back or supply feedback by posting photographs on social media, offering social commentary and curating their own exhibitions. The museum appears more accessible as multiple publics incorporate contemporary technologies into the flow of their meaning-making practices (Black 2005; Simon 2010), in effect bringing to mind visualisations of a democratic and engaging museum experience.

The Habermasian public sphere serves as a fulcrum for understanding the museum's relationship with technology because it is produced by publicity while also shaping citizenry. Publicity is used as a 'procedural substitute' for 'authority' because it creates an illusion of a participatory public made up of 'conspiring subjects' who appear to be powerful, ruling particular outcomes in or out, but who in essence lack real authority (Dean 2002: 162). Images on social media feeds demonstrate the multiple ways in which the museum is democratised in its more interactive and participatory formation. There is a general sense among museum professionals that technology can create forms of valued dialogue, which in turn afford intimate relationships with the audience. Yet the experience of making the museum more accessible and searchable using the digital opens up new questions about the sociopolitical function of publicity and can carry an assumption that the digital platforms that mediate this content are free of algorithmic manipulation (van Dijck 2013). Following Habermas's logic, it is not unreasonable to port the idea of publicity to the interactive and participatory museum of today. For one thing, digital media devices contribute to how the museum is understood and imagined.

The MONA 'O' case study in Chapter 3 highlights that the forms of personalisation that tailor the experience of the institution to the individual are drawn upon by museum workers and discussed as a way to flatten the authority of the institution. In industry blogs and in at least a dozen interviews for this book, cultural workers reiterated the importance of understanding user behaviour and integrating it into their everyday activities. This is forcing museums to rethink how they go about fulfilling their mission statements. The ways in which the museum defines and communicates with its visitors are increasingly dependent on complex forms of data analysis and machine learning.

Rather than spending time physically within the institution, social interaction doesn't need to be limited by spatiality but can be carried out remotely. The user who is located 'here' is able to experience a sense of physical proximity with a museum that is located 'there'. This has ramifications for the museum because it becomes beholden to the expectation that devices and digital platforms will mediate public experience. Rather than museums taking on the attributes of media platforms – which is, of course, taking place – museum visitors are essentially connecting with the museum on their smartphones.

What is the importance of large cultural datasets being housed on media platforms and of shifting understandings about how audiences engage with these institutions? Nieborg and Poell (2018: 4279) argue that media platforms have brought about 'new economic and institutional configurations of cultural production, leaving "content producers" in a "position of dependency"'. Because digital media platforms are regarded as essential, there is a transformation of cultural strategies and ways of working to align with the 'sociotechnical system' of the media platform. To apply Nieborg and Poell's (2018: 4278) argument to the museum, its structure shifts from a 'two-sided market', whereby the audience interacts directly with the institution, to a 'multi-sided platform' configuration in which media platforms work as 'aggregators and mediators' that 'are able to exert significant control over the institutional relationships with end-users and complementors'.

For the museum, this can involve cultural collections being made accessible to audiences, who then engage with a collection by circulating content on social media. Cultural and social audiences perform the work of documenting and sharing cultural experiences, which in turn inform online data collection and advertising. Simply by configuring collection spaces for on-site social media photography and by building an online collection designed to be shareable, the museum is plugged into the platform economy. Mike Pepi (2014), an independent arts writer who covers art, culture and technology, has famously argued that the museum is adjusting to the logic of the database, its artefacts transformed into digital formats in online archives of open access collections. Institutions are appearing to act less as storehouses of physical objects than as collections of images and data, where cultural content is reformulated with the aim that multiple publics will connect with content and engage in activity on social networks (see Figure 4.1).

Similarly, Andrejevic (2007: 94) uses the term 'ubiquity' to capture the widening 'digital enclosure' that has been brought about by interactive devices and platforms. While providing convenience and customisation to users, these have reconfigured engagement with the physical world. From his perspective, ubiquity refers to the endowment 'of physical spaces with the interactive character of the internet', by enabling people to access 'information (such as the directions or movie listings) while simultaneously narrowcasting information about their movements and preferences to those who own and operate the means of interaction' (Andrejevic 2007: 94). This may involve interactive spaces replicating 'complex media systems' and/

Figure 4.1 Museum experiences are now both virtual and physical, where digital technologies can enrich the museum experience and provide a host of new opportunities for visitors to engage with collections.

Source: Image taken at Holoverse – Dinosaur World in Queensland, Australia.

or being used by participants in such a way that they use their labour – for example, tweeting locations and uploading photographs to the web that echo the forms of visibility and surveillance common to 'digital enclosures' (Andrejevic 2007: 94) (see Figure 4.2).

Scott McQuire (2008: 107) echoes this sentiment, arguing that 'public agency is expressed through media consumption in public space' and 'social interaction' that takes place via 'complex media systems' creating 'collective assemblies'. Each of these scholars reinforces an understanding of the museum as a space that is increasingly understood as engaged with through digital means. To arrive at an understanding of the transformation of today's institutions in line with new distributions of cultural and economic power, we first have to explore the various approaches of museum workers and think about what they mean for the current and future configuration of museums and their visitors.

What does the use of social media by museums and their visitors mean for twenty-first-century institutions – in particular, the use of instant responses

Figure 4.2 Visitor smartphones and apps are an important resource, providing layers of additional content such as music and artist interviews to enhance the museum experience.

Source: Museum of Contemporary Art Australia's mca.art Signage, 2019, featuring: Guan Wei, Feng Shui (detail), 2004, acrylic on composite board, Museum of Contemporary Art, donated through the Australian Government's Cultural Gifts Program by Cromwell Diversified Property Trust, 2017, image courtesy and © the artist and Museum of Contemporary Art Australia.

and forms of automated dialogue which demonstrate new communication norms that coincide with the rise of the media platforms and the smartphone? Drawing on examples, the aim is to consider the alignment of the museum operations with new market arrangements and to carefully examine shifts in the platformised participation of cultural audiences.

Platformised participation

Traditional pre-nineteenth-century forms of exhibition-displays primarily involved communication with audiences around a set institutional narratives presented by curators and displayed in signage. Over the past decade, a number of museums have been working towards constructing a more egalitarian environment using digital tools. There is further emphasis on becoming 'engaged' with multiple publics who want to 'interact' with the museum and digital platforms that then facilitate that interactivity. Media platforms become the lens through which that cultural interactivity is imagined. Media-based experiences are fundamentally integrated into cultural workers' ideas, images and concepts of the museum and the envisioning of the sociocultural conditions in which it operates. In this process, the institution must present audiences with opportunities for content creation and exchange. As one international expert who conducts social media training regularly with museum staff explained:

> In the twenty-first century, museums need to adopt a less authoritative tone and use social media to regularly communicate with audiences by displaying multiple perspectives and points of view. . . . Museums expect to talk to people but they don't expect them to talk back. So, the public goes well so we won't talk [back] to you then. And now they [the museums] are going but they aren't talking to us? When you do a hashtag you can prove to the public how good it [the museum] was [at communicating with users] and show how much they loved it.

By connecting with audiences using digital networks, the museum becomes a part of the promotional culture of the platform. The media infrastructure creates an opportunity to deepen the connection between the institution and the visitor. Museum hashtags and images shared in spaces such as Instagram are popular with audiences and institutions because they allow audiences to see themselves participating in a cultural experience while promoting awareness about an exhibit. Museum visitors take pictures of objects, at times using artefacts as a backdrop for a selfie. The same expert explained:

> This shift towards engaging with objects using smartphones has required new ways of thinking by the museum, people want to take pictures in museums . . . now they all have selfie stations. People didn't used to let people take photographs in the museum but now they have changed policy. [In the past] they would be . . . concerned about copyright and I would say move the pictures to a different room and let the people take pictures of everything else.

As this reflection neatly captures, the tendency of audiences to repackage and circulate museum imagery on social media has involved a reinvention of institutional approaches and exhibits. Social media create opportunities for audience visibility, and the publicity practices of visitors encourage visitation. Museum spaces are purposely reconfigured for audiences to use smartphones in photography-friendly environments. This is beneficial for the museum, as it gains broad public attention through the dissemination of images and hashtags online. Activities such as #askacurator day – an initiative that began in 2010 on Twitter, which was designed to encourage people who might not otherwise feel comfortable asking questions about objects – demonstrates to museum audiences the accessibility of the institutional specialists (Richardson 2020).

Writing as an expert in predictive market intelligence, Colleen Dilenschneider (2013) states on her website 'Know your own Bone', an online resource for cultural organisations, that '42% of individuals using social media expect answers to the questions that they ask online within one hour – whether or not it is Ask a Curator Day'. From her perspective, #askacurator day is a 'symbolic day for the museum community – and the visitor-serving organizations that made a coordinated effort to show their willingness to be receptive to audiences in real time'. As institutions respond to questions ranging from 'Is your museum haunted?' right through to 'How are you making your museum relevant to young people?', they demonstrate a commitment to providing equal public access to collections. Visitors experience the museum as media streams that evolve rapidly in real time.

As early as 2016, director of digital and emerging media from the Cooper Hewitt in New York, Micah Walter, predicted that media platforms would be critical in the targeting and personalisation of museum communication. In a post on the institution's 'Labs' page, he discusses 'Object Phone', an initiative from three years earlier that allowed users to call and text different objects in the collection:

> I'd love to see Object Phone make its way onto the platform of your choice. I think this is a critical next step. SMS is great, and available to nearly anyone with a cell phone, but apps like FB Messenger, WhatsApp, and LINE have the ability to connect a service like Object Phone with a captive audience, all over the world. I think institutions like museums have a great opportunity in the chatbot space. If anything, it represents a new way to broaden our reach and connect with people on the platforms they are already using. What's more interesting to me is that chatbots themselves represent a way to interact with people that is by its very nature, bi-directional.
>
> (Walter 2016)

As Walter demonstrates, there is a perceived objective for museums to configure their communication within digital networks. Curators and education departments have a task to play, as do computer scientists and other digital experts.

Since that early prediction, machine-driven forms of communication have proved to be a growing part of how institutions maintain contact with audiences (Gaia, Boiano and Borda 2019). Anne Frank House in Amsterdam, as a result of a partnership with Facebook Netherlands, launched a messenger chatbot in 2017 to achieve its mission of 'bringing the life story of Anne Frank to the attention of as many people as possible worldwide' (Anne Frank House 2007). The chatbot performs a form of cultural mediation because it takes on the responsibility for fostering a relationship between the museum and the online visitor, as it is able to be incorporated into their online social world. Anne Frank House describes the purpose of the chatbot on its website:

> It is a way to reach people all over the world and inform them about Anne Frank's life and warn them for the risks and effects of racism and discrimination. That is ultimately what new technologies should be used for: to better our lives and concur the challenges society faces.
>
> (Anne Frank House 2017)

Highlighting the potential of the technology, the chatbot effectively achieves the museum's aim by transforming a fixed past into a dynamic format that promotes new understandings by creating an open space for dialogue – albeit between a machine and a human. The AI provides highly personalised responses to user queries about the story of Anne's life as well as practical visitor information. Able to operate 24 hours a day, the technology (at least to a certain extent) stands in for a docent or curator broadening access to the museum and its message. In this context, the chatbot brings the museum beyond its physical boundaries to an online space where conversation can be repackaged into a social media format. The self-learning AI alters traditional power relations by transforming the character of Anne Frank into a digital avatar of sorts. It enhances the quality of engagement with the museum while being tasked with providing accurate historical information that will assist with reducing anti-Semitism. Especially targeted at young audiences, it operates as a tool of resistance against religious discrimination and performs a sociopolitical role. The chatbot prevents the spread of misinformation through the provision of easily accessible accurate information. The lack of human oversight of the chatbot technology makes it a highly effective mediation tool for the museum because it is able to respond to queries in real time.

As a digital collections and open access specialist at the Harvard Library Innovation Lab, Kelly Fitzpatrick (2017) argues that heritage bots can be beneficial to 'offer a way to passively interface with collection content for inclusion in a larger stream of media – providing an alternative user experience while directing users to the content's original source'. The Cooper Hewitt, Victoria and Albert Museum, Brooklyn Museum and Tate are among the many museums that now use chatbots to randomly tweet objects from the collection during the day in order to broaden access to collections. The concept that objects are randomly selected from the collection upsets some of the traditional hierarchies of high art and positions the museum as participatory and democratic. Twitter prompts the museum to convert its collection into media content, which in turn invites audiences into the dialogue.

Although not always affiliated with a particular institution, bots can provide another channel through which museums can connect users with objects, in a sense providing broader visibility of the collection as a result of its random object selection. These Twitter accounts constitute key players in the social media ecosystem of an institution because of their ability to respond to a range of questions in real time. It is important, however, to remember that Twitter bots are an extension of some of the thinking that has been at play in museums for some time. As early as 2011, the Tate developed the 'Magic Tate Ball', an app that, when shaken, activated an algorithm that relied on data from the user's GPS data, the date, time, weather and noise levels to select a specific artwork for the user to view in the exhibition or collection. At the time of the app's release, Anne Burton, Tate Media's head of content and creative director, said:

> I love the serendipity of discovering art through Magic Tate Ball – you never know which artwork you're going to get. We aimed it at both existing Tate fans and new audiences who are interested in a more playful experience than cultural institutions typically offer.
>
> (Templeton 2012)

A particular form of reasoning appears to be embedded into the practices of cultural workers who embrace digital media in their daily practices in order to expose collections to multiple publics. This shift reflects potentialities for new forms and structures of power in the wake of networked societies. The museum's top-down centralised mode of authority and communication is decentralised as it is forced to adopt new modes of content production. In the case of the Magic Tate Ball, users' ambient data are drawn from mobile phones as a source of information to be mined by the museum to facilitate new forms of interactivity.

There is an effort to use the smartphone to integrate culture into the user's daily life in the context of participatory culture (Jenkins 2019). In many cases, this involves users performing a simple practice or actions that can be analysed. The platform works to shape notions of culture and art by making objects available. The objects themselves hold cultural value, which to a certain extent is appropriated by the user who by performing simple actions that then incorporate it into their daily life – often through forms of social media sharing.

Rather than a model of human-to-human communication, and of a culture of semi-permanent and permanent exhibits, these examples demonstrate a new typology of museum that involves embracing peer sharing and real-time automation. The museum visitor engages with the museum using the tools of media platforms to interact with objects and express themselves. This next section explores why this approach to engaging with culture supports the data-processing efforts of media platforms.

How the platformisation of the museum is driven by the need for data

In its basic form, platformisation utilises a cloud-based platform to host the value offered to customers or audience. As a relatable explanation for museums, it is when the museum pays for a service to host its online archive, taking advantage of the features provided by the service, such as free data storage, an inbuilt search engine, analytics feedback, collaboration, video playback and photo library applications. As an example of this relationship, particular attention is paid to the GAC, which is home to collections from over 2,000 partner institutions globally to explore the recent move towards engaging with artworks and objects in a platform-based environment (Google Arts and Culture Institute 2020). Positioned as a not-for-profit initiative, GAC is designed to preserve and bring the world's art and culture online, rendering it 'accessible to anyone, anywhere' (Google Arts and Culture 2020) in fitting with the organisation's mission to 'organise the world's information and make it universally accessible and useful' (Google 2018) (see Figure 4.3). The web interface and app are free of any commercial agenda apart from the potential benefit of Google using the cultural collections housed on the website as a machine learning training set. Based on this large and globally distributed collection, the AI systems can then use these data to distinguish patterns across the digitised images, such as facial features, as well as analyse scenes in artworks and evaluate different painting styles.

Michelle Luo, the GAC product manager who created a number of GAC's existing innovations, explains that these experiments are designed to explore what is possible when you combine art and technology because 'AI can be a powerful tool in the hands of artists, museums, and curators to create new experience and unlock art for everyone, and we aim to connect not only these artists with the latest technologies, but also everyone who has a camera in their pocket' (Saunders 2020). On the website, the experiments are described as 'playful tools' that were made possible through the

68 *From museum to platform*

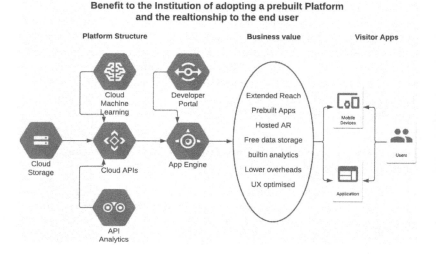

Figure 4.3 This diagram demonstrates the relationship between a GAC-type platform and the end user, showing the benefit to the institution of creating this relationship.

work of 'Creative Coders' (Google 2020). This is a feature of the website, where collections are used to trial different contemporary ways of accessing culture from completing a crossword to colouring famous paintings. GAC is similar to other media platforms in that it invites users to experiment with cultural content, which in many cases is provided in a format that encourages users to distribute these outputs across their social media networks. However, unlike other media platforms, there is no clear commercial brand agenda.

After downloading the free GAC app, users are encouraged to engage with objects within the collections using smartphones in a range of ways. Launched as a new feature within the app in 2020, Art Transfer demonstrates the capacity of neural networks – a series of algorithms that mimic a human brain – to create unique visuals. The in-app experiment allows users to load an image and select from around 40 AR art filters to create a media object that can be shared on social media. Opening the camera menu within the GAC app users can select 'Art Transfer' and take a photo using their phone or upload an existing image (see Figure 4.4). Selecting from filters inspired by the styles of artists ranging from Vincent van Gogh to Leonardo da Vinci, a filter is applied to the photograph by the user. An automated

From museum to platform   69

Figure 4.4 Users can take photographs of themselves using Art Transfer on the GAC app, which applies an art filter to create an output that places the user into iconic artworks.

Source: Image produced using the Google Arts and Culture app.

morphing of the image into the style of the selected artwork is generated, which enables an entirely new image to be created.

While the positioning of the original artwork is preserved, the artwork informs the colour and technique depicted in the output. In a sense, this feature is reproducing those similar to media platforms such as Snapchat and TikTok, where users play with a series of pre-supplied filters. The juxtaposed outputs are then made available for circulation and social media commentary online across a user's peer networks (Collie and Wilson-Barnao 2020). This is in keeping with other forms of interactive participation experienced on media platforms where augmented images of users are compressed with advertisements and distributed in peer networks (Hawker and Carah 2020: 3).

The app optimises the existing participation of museum visitors, who are already accustomed to taking photos of themselves and producing imagery using digital tools but accelerates this turn by ensuring that the outputs are immediately shareable on media platforms. The app generates a novel form of participation that is less about access to collections or speaking back to the institution to ask questions. Instead, the collection becomes not something to appreciate or interpret but rather something to play with. A piece of code can be used to augment the user's own identity, and therefore the collection begins to circulate through social media in new ways in the form of augmented faces rather than the original object.

GAC invites a particular type of engagement with culture, one that is playful and geared towards the production and distribution of promotional material. On its blog, Google describes the technology as kicking 'off a unique algorithmic recreation of your photo inspired by the specific art style you have chosen' (Luo 2020). There is a collapsing of cultural content housed within the collection with forms of everyday forms of mediation. Objects in the collection become available to users less as artworks in their own right and more as novel lenses to be applied to a user's own likeness. In this iteration, the museum visitor shifts from a mode of engagement where they view artworks within a physical institution to one in which they interact with objects online by taking selfies and using art filters. On one level, the AR filter provides the user with greater creative control in relation to their interaction with the artwork by allowing them to select from the pre-supplied filters, but on another, the aesthetics and logics of the platform are ported into the cultural engagement. Rather than being viewed as static and to be consumed in its own right, the artwork transforms into something to be interacted with and altered. The user is central to this notion and the digital tools provided determine the scope of what is possible and what is not, creating new norms about how the culture is experienced and shared.

GAC's visitors are not just viewers, but instead need to perform a practice to enable online content sharing. Culture becomes a design overlay that is adjusted to enable the creation of an image that is an expression of the user, which is then posted and shared across different social media forums. A blending of cultural objects with user identities within a range of overlapping media platforms takes place, where the poster acquires social capital because of their engagement with culture. Reappropriated artworks then circulate within a broader social context, where cultural audiences go about what Andrejevic (2002) describes as the work of being watched. Individuals give up their labour to share content within digital enclosures, where they experience 'increasingly pervasive and comprehensive forms of high tech monitoring' (Andrejevic 2002: 231). While accelerated prevalence of promotional practices such as this is easily regarded as a natural development with some residual benefits to the institutions themselves, this perspective fails to consider how the logic of publicity has become central to the museum. A particular form of publicity is enacted that is synonymous with the creation and distribution of content. Artworks gain enhanced accessibility as a result of their open and performative use but remain synonymous with the platformised participation of audiences.

Conclusion

As the interviews, examples and industry documents reveal, the push towards the platformisation of the museum is motivated by a desire to establish new conditions for maintaining and developing relationships with audiences. This is driven by the need for access, participation and personalisation, which involves embracing digital methods to align the museum with the contemporary practices of media platforms. There is a clear disruption of old ways of thinking about visitors and a move towards a view that the publicity outputs of users are beneficial – which in many ways they are.

Significantly, museum objects are placed into everyday spaces on social media, where users encounter objects within streams of unrelated content. That is not to suggest that museums haven't already been experimenting with how to incorporate technologies into their daily practices for some time. The Tate launched the IK Prize in 2016 in a partnership with Microsoft that involved challenging creatives to incorporate AI into their collection (Tate 2016). Instead, the issue is to highlight ways to think about how the museum is enacted through digital intermediaries and the forms of publicness they bring about. Without doubt, there can be significant benefits to the data insights that locative media provide to collections. The Australian Museum, as a result of a collaboration with IBM iX, is using a specially created app that allows the general public to record frog sounds onto a database that, by drawing on GPS technology, maps frog populations nationally (IBM 2017). Museum experts can then identify the amphibian type based upon the sounds it makes in order to gain critical insight into the health of populations and their associated habitat. Rather than top-down research conducted only by experts, crowd-sourced knowledge is acquired in an emerging and multilayered world where the monitoring abilities of citizens help to solve complex problems. The smartphone becomes a resource that provides multiple publics with opportunities to assist institutions in fulfilling their missions and vision statements. Technology such as this app signifies new approaches.

In contrast with museums of old, the operating model of media platforms works to datafy this content in order to commodify it (van Dijck, Poell and De Waal 2018: 31–46). As a result, algorithms have gained a powerful stake in how the museum looks and works. The following chapter turns to consider media platforms acting as gatekeepers to, and as both producers and facilitators of, cultural content. In some instances, an entire museum experience can take place within a media platform. While this transformation goes hand in hand with a full suite of benefits, it persuades attention to the museum's increased dependency upon the platforms and structures of the digital age and raises new ethical concerns about automated technologies taking on social and historical concerns.

References

Andrejevic, Mark (2002). The work of being watched: Interactive media and the exploitation of self-disclosure. *Critical Studies in Media Communication*, 19(2): 230–48.
Andrejevic, Mark (2007). *iSpy: Surveillance and Power in the Interactive Era*. Lawrence, KS: University Press of Kansas.
Anne Frank House (2017). Anne frank house launches bot for messenger. Retrieved from www.annefrank.org/en/about-us/news-and-press/news/2017/3/21/anne-frank-house-launches-bot-messenger.
Anne Frank House (2007). Anne frank house annual report. Retrieved from www.annefrank.org/en/about-us/what-we-do/annual-report-2017/organisation/organisation-and-mission/#:~:text=The%20Anne%20Frank%20House%20is,with%20the%20aim%20of%20raising.
Barrett, Jennifer (2011). *Museums and the Public Sphere*. London: Wiley-Blackwell.
Bennett, Tony (1995). *The Birth of the Museum: History, Theory, Politics*. London: Routledge.
Bishop, Claire (2012). *Artificial Hells: Participatory Art and the Politics of Spectatorship*. New York: Verso.
Black, Graham (2005). *The Engaging Museum: Developing Museums for Visitor Involvement*. New York: Routledge.
Bourriaud, Nicolas (2002). *Esthétique relationelle (Relational Aesthetics)*. Dijon: Les Presses du Réel.
Collie, Natalie and Wilson-Barnao, Caroline (2020). Playing with TikTok: Algorithmic culture and the future of creative work. In Greg Hearn (ed), *The Future of Creative Work*. London: Edward Elgar, pp. 172–88.
Dean, Jodi (2002). *Publicity's Secret: How Technoculture Capitalizes on Democracy*. New York: Cornell University Press.
Dilenschneider, Colleen (2013). *Know your own bone*. Retrieved from https://www.colleendilen.com/2013/09/25/the-true-benefit-of-ask-a-curator-day-and-why-it-is-not-what-museums-think/.
Fitzpatrick, Kelly (2017). Medium. Retrieved from https://medium.com/berkman-klein-center/anatomy-of-a-museum-twitter-bot-2311d81de243.

Gaia, Giuliano, Boiano, Stefania and Borda, Ann (2019). Engaging museum visitors with AI: The case of chatbots. In Tula Giannini and Jonathan Bowen (eds), *Museums and Digital Culture: New Perspectives and Research*. London: Springer, pp. 309–29.

Google (2018). Maximise access to information. Retrieved from www.google.com/search/howsearchworks/mission.

Google (2020). Art & culture experiments. Retrieved from https://experiments.with google.com/collection/arts-culture.

Google Arts and Culture (2020). Bringing the world's art and culture online for everyone. Retrieved from https://about.artsandculture.google.com.

Templeton, Ben (2012). Mobile culture and the magic Tate ball. *The Guardian*, 16 July. Retrieved from www.theguardian.com/culture-professionals-network/culture-professionals-blog/2012/jul/16/mobile-culture-magic-tate-ball-app.

Habermas, Jurgen (1989 [1962]). *The Structural Transformation of the Public Sphere*. Trans. Thomas Burger and Frederick Lawrence. Cambridge, MA: MIT Press.

Hawker, Kiah and Carah, Nicholas (2020). Snapchat's augmented reality brand culture: Sponsored filters and lenses as digital piecework. *Continuum*. doi:10.1080/10304312.2020.1827370.

Heumann Gurian, Elaine (2006). *Civilizing the Museum*. London: Routledge.

Hooper-Greenhill, Eilean (1992). *Museums and the Shaping of Knowledge*. New York: Routledge.

IBM (2017). Australian museum FrogID: How Australians are lending their ears to help native frogs. Retrieved from www.ibm.com/services/ibmix/case-studies/_australian-museum.html.

Jenkins, Henry (2019). *Participatory Culture*. New York: Polity Press.

Luo, Michelle (2020). Transform your photo in the style of an iconic artist. *The Keyword*. Retrieved from https://blog.google/outreach-initiatives/arts-culture/transform-your-photo-style-iconic-artist.

McClellan, Andrew (1994). *Inventing the Louvre: Art, Politics, and the Origins of the Modern Museum in Eighteenth-century Paris*. London: Cambridge University Press.

McQuire, Scott (2008). *The media city: media, architecture and urban space*. London: Sage.

Nieborg, David and Poell, Thomas (2018). The platformisation of cultural production: Theorizing the contingent cultural commodity. *New Media & Society*, 20(11): 4275–92.

Pepi, Mike (2014). Is the museum a database? Institutional conditions in net utopia. *E-flux*, 60. Retrieved from www.e-flux.com/journal/60/61026/is-a-museum-a-database-institutional-conditions-in-net-utopia.

Poell, Thomas, Nieborg, David and van Dijck, Jose (2019). Platformisation. *Internet Policy Review*, 8(4), doi:10.14763/2019.4.1425.

Richardson, Jim (2020). Ask a curator day returns on September 16, 2020. *Museum Next*. Retrieved from www.museumnext.com/article/ask-a-curator-returns-on-september-16th-2020.

Sandell, Richard (1998). Museums as agents of social inclusion. *Museum Management and Curatorship*, 17(4): 401–18.

Saunders, Tanner (2020). This new Google feature transforms your photos into art inspired by legends like Frida Kahlo and Vincent van Gogh. *Travel & Leisure*. Retrieved from www.travelandleisure.com/culture-design/visual-arts/new-google-feature-art-transfer.

Simon, Nina (2010). *The Participatory Museum*. Santa Cruz, CA: Creative Commons. Retrieved from www.participatorymuseum.org.

Tate (2016). IK Prize. Retrieved from https://www.tate.org.uk/about-us/projects/ik-prize.

van Dijck, Jose (2013). Facebook and the engineering of connectivity: A multilayered approach to social media platforms. *Convergence: The International Journal of Research into New Media Technologies*, 19(2): 141–55.

van Dijck, Jose, Poell, Thomas and De Waal, Martijn (2018). *The Platform Society: Public Values in a Connective World*. London: Oxford University Press.

Walter, Micah (2016). *Object Phone: The Continued Evolution of a Little Chatbot*. Cooper Hewitt Labs. Retrieved from https://labs.cooperhewitt.org/2016/object-phone-the-continued-evolution-of-a-little-chatbot.

Weil, Stephen E. (2002). *Making Museums Matter*. New York: Smithsonian Press.

5 Negotiating museums as platforms

Introduction

The enmeshing of powerful platforms and cultural institutions in the digital space has the potential to alter the forms of access provided by the museum. In many instances, digital media devices and platforms can advance the public value of the museum as an open approach to sharing data and content. It allows information about artefacts to be centralised. Collections can be tailored better to audiences. Audiences can curate collections. Users can share artefacts, and cultural dialogue is encouraged online. For these reasons, digital technologies help the museum to operate as a robust public sphere. This shift in improved online access has been accelerated by the impact of COVID-19 on institutions and their aspiration to remain viable when the doors are closed to visitors. The move to addressing cultural audiences as 'prosumers' and device users has altered not only the museum's ideas about how to regard their multiple publics (and how these publics view themselves) but also their overall engagement with these spaces. Followers on social media can translate into an instant engaged audience that can be accessed and listened to. Posting images and sharing content on platforms is a legitimate way in which everyday audiences now connect with the museum (Budge and Burness 2018) and share their experiences (Carah 2014). To interrogate this view and provide an insider perspective, the reflections of cultural workers are drawn upon to estimate the impact of reconfiguring of the museum's social architecture to media platforms in a shift that has been exacerbated further by COVID-19. As iterated in Chapter 3, unlike traditional museum experiences where the artefacts and artworks offer few opportunities for audience involvement, institutions are reconfiguring their exhibits and spaces to accommodate new forms of interactive participation to appeal to the on-site visitor and remote web-enabled visitors. Jia Jia Fei, digital director at the Jewish Museum in New York, explained in a TEDx Talk that 'in the pre-digital photography era, the

DOI: 10.4324/9780429298691-5

message was: this is what I'm seeing. I have seen. And today, the message is: I was there. I came, I saw, and I selfied' (Raphelson 2017).

An elementary but widespread example of institutions using this form of engagement is of artists working with cultural organisations to create selfie booths and digital stations located within the museum or gallery. The artworks used in these environments are often malleable, and they are packaged in a way that will enable the accommodation of the promotional logics of social media platforms by creating opportunities for audiences to post content online. The audience is invited to 'do something' that acts as a catalyst for photography. Often the individual can then personalise the image by adding effects or comments, tagging friends and making their location known to others. In this way, objects are then placed within the narrative of the social poster's media stream, where the individual gains attention with their followers and network as it circulates in a transient 'attention economy' (Simon 1971: 40–41). The focus of selfie booths and digital stations is to generate a curated setting for the user to personalise their engagement with the institution on social media platforms. Audiences become creators of content – prosumers – whose individual subjectivities are incorporated into artwork.

Orchestrated public activities such as Ask a Curator Day and the positioning of selfie booths on-site reinforce the demonstrated capacity of the museum to use publicity practices to attract audiences. In addition, advertisers have contributed to a publicity-driven culture, where it is common for people to use filters and other branded digital tools to express themselves within social networks where they share imagery. There is a sense that the audience gains heightened creative control through the distribution of content across multiple platforms (Drotner and Schrøder 2014; Henning 2006; Hsi 2003; Kidd 2011; Villaespesa and French 2019). In this context, publicity describes a multifaceted model in which visitors exert influence over how the institution attracts potential audiences and in turn how it measures its impact on its audience. This publicity-driven mode of viewing not only has implications for how people see themselves engaging with culture but generates affordances in dispersing the museum across myriad social spaces. This mode of engagement has helped the museum to occupy attention on the internet and can function as a glimpse into how its visibility increases on social media.

A new museum architecture

The case studies throughout this book describe and demonstrate the museum being reimagined and reshaped within the framework of platform media, rendering the museum, its objects and its audiences more visible. Some museums are hesitant to fully embrace platformisation, while others see it as mission critical. In response to this change, university museum studies departments are launching new programmes that incorporate skill sets in digital analytics, audience research and digital curation (Lopes 2020: 125). The digital strategies of the Tate, British Museum and Van Gogh Museum, among many, highlight a long-term commitment by larger cultural institutions to employ staff adequately skilled in using new technology. A director of engagement at a large state museum considered the concept of the museum's shifting organisational structure:

> The role of the curator [expert] is definitely changing but their skill set and their expectations are relevant and in fact more relevant than they have ever been. We encourage them to all be in the media, to be contributing their ideas, their work, the things they discover. So any new things that we discover we make sure we author them with Wikipedia entries.

While the examples of major museums are worthy of media attention, the platformisation of the museum cannot be regarded as only shaping large institutions. Small, private and independent establishments without in-house expertise or the ability to invest in up-to-date equipment, software and staff training are at a distinct disadvantage. As Vermeeren and Calvi (2017: 114) point out, small museums can also be reliant upon older volunteers with limited technical competency in areas such as social media engagement, content curation and digital asset management. Even with these limitations, smaller institutions stand to benefit from having an online presence that will broaden audiences and interest. Crucially, museums find themselves negotiating complex choices that entail sophisticated technical literacy. While cultural workers may already be comfortable using social media and digitising content, the integration of advanced AI tools can juxtapose the time and expense of working in-house on a project against seeking out partnerships (Villaespesa and French 2019: 106). This is most noticeable when museum professionals acknowledge limitations to their digital in-house expertise and the restraints that limit exhibition development, which can push them towards less autonomous modes of production. As a director of a regional museum explained:

> We have been built as a digital space. The strategic issue for us is how do we keep cutting edge. So as you know being digital has its own set of challenges. For us how do we keep up with the hardware, the software, to cost effectively find new content.

The shift towards platformised context can be unevenly distributed among institutions. For many institutions, it can mean upskilling existing staff and the creation of new forms of employment. For other institutions, traditional job definitions and organisational structures are shifting – albeit slowly – to accommodate curators, docents, specialists and educators using digital tools. Articulating that expert knowledge is irreplaceable, the same director of engagement at a large state museum contends that most curators are swamped and suggests that 'it is a matter of changing the technology to assist'. In this case, there is acknowledgement that technology extends the museum's social value by actively generating different types of digital connection, thus furthering the institution's civic purpose. However, being limited by their financial ability to facilitate new initiatives also incentivises them to seek out partnerships with technology specialists and aligned technology outside of the industry.

Museums as platforms

The impact of the norms of media platforms upon the museum is rarely a point of contention. Only on occasion does a news story capture instances of disruption, such as when a French art collective Obvious created an AI that generated an artwork, *Portrait of Edmond de Belamy* (see Figure 5.1), which sold for $432,000 at Christie's (Hitti 2018). Or, as occurred on another occasion, when a Blockchain museum for digital art, Wunder, provided an open-source interface for artists and collectors to list individual and collective works for sale, renegotiating the function of commercial galleries globally (Aitken 2019).

The media primarily speculates on how AI will generate art in the future or on how digitisation democratises culture. Institutions incorporate digital practices with an understanding that everyone benefits. The notion of museums as platforms is a provocation that highlights the extent to which various forms of mediatisation now sustain multiple audiences and work to draw attention to shifting cultural practices at a time when data are valuable to companies that sell things and promote products. Instead of museums standing alone and separate, and media platforms acting as conduits, museums are being subsumed within a series of overlapping digital enclosures.

In this way, we can identify potentially two versions of a platform-based museum playing out. The first involves a museum (or museum collective) owning and operating the platform. The second is where museums embrace a private media platform presiding over the infrastructure that facilitates audience engagement. The Europeana and the Rijksmuseum collections are examples of the first version of museum platform configuration. The infrastructure that delivers digital access to objects and exhibitions is publicly owned and made available as a result of a sustained government

Figure 5.1 This image, *Portrait of Edmond de Belamy*, by art collective Obvious, was generated by AI and was sold at auction by Christie's for $432,000.

Source: Image by Obvious.

investment. Europeana matches this description of one expression of a platform. Financed through the European Union, this online infrastructure provides digital access to over 3,000 institutions across Europe. Similarly, the RijksStudio is operated by the Rijksmuseum, the Dutch National Museum, and makes available to the public over 125,000 digital images of artefacts.

Both these online repositories provide copyright-free imagery for users but do not receive any direct financial return from user engagement with the collection. On RijksStudio, users are encouraged to recreate artworks that can then be used for private or commercial purposes. Here, the museum maintains its own brand and remains relatively free from the profitability frameworks guiding commercially operated media. This model is aligned with open platform-based environments such as Creative Commons, which is designed to enhance the educational and creative use of collections. Users engage with digital replicas of the 'real thing', where they gain knowledge and experience artefacts that can enrich their understanding. Page views, comments, likes and downloads of images housed in the collection and their use in spaces such as Wikipedia evidence the sustainability and popularity of digital imagery. Importantly, these collections represent an attempt by museums to maintain control over their digital transformation.

As outlined, the second version of the museum platform includes institutions that are dependent primarily upon privately owned media platforms to deliver collection access and do not own or possess a conduit to a developed digital infrastructure for audience engagement. Because of the lack of infrastructure, these institutions are reliant upon the media infrastructures of third parties that can provide the key interface for collection access. While it is a not-for-profit initiative, GAC is an example of this type of platform arrangement, as it generates value for Google by bringing together cultural heritage into one digital interface (Pesce, Neirotti and Paolucci 2019). Museums opt in to make their collections and data available because the use of collection content within these spaces extends the institution's research, educational and interactive activities. To facilitate audience interaction, media platforms recalibrate collection content into a format that renders objects more interactive, malleable and participatory. The brand of the museum is strengthened by the reuse and distribution of artefacts using new forms of technology; however, there is a structural reformulation of the museum that reinforces the influence and concentration of corporate control over what might otherwise be identified as public resources.

It is important to acknowledge that cultural institutions are experimenting with many forms of collection access, and that some straddle both modalities. The Rijksmuseum, for instance, has collections hosted on GAC, Creative Commons/Flickr and its own platform. Some institutions in this group use a hybrid cloud model, where they own the abstracted software layer of mobile app, digital gallery and search functionality, therefore retaining control and licensing, but outsource the computing power and data storage to a cloud infrastructure provider such as Amazon Web Services or Microsoft (Azure Cloud). In either instance, museums digitise their collections either independently or in collaboration with media platforms to broaden access to the collection. The participatory nature of the platform and the social networks it builds up create dynamic social encounters for audiences, and after the artefacts are uploaded to a chosen platform they become searchable within the ecosystem of overlapping digital platforms. The key to viability is a media platform that generates economic value from data, which then becomes useful in different contexts from its original source in the form of internet searches, shares, feedback metrics and audience identification and profiling.

Despite these similarities, each configuration of the platform-based museum should be understood differently. This is because the sociotechnical features of each environment vary. The first platform arrangement promotes a structural transformation that is the key to achieving the institutional aspiration of access. It fosters a culture of social cohesion and inclusion and is underpinned by the delivery of these museum services. The museum drives this mode of innovation with the aim of ensuring that its resources are used appropriately. The second platform version also engages with the prevailing model of digital platforms. Yet a co-dependency on media platforms ensues whereby the museum acquires its value through the repeated use of content, which in turn enhances the museum's social worth and value. The uses of digital tools in this context triggers new issues for museums, both in terms of their not-for-profit frameworks and their alignment with the commercial opportunities offered by digital data. The model for attribution is relatively loose, with a platform like Creative Commons asking politely for you to 'Credit the Creator' (see Figure 5.2).

American political theorist and academic Jodi Dean is helpful in conceptualising the participation of museum visitors as coextensive with platform media and offers the concept of 'communicative capitalism' to understand how the 'open architecture' of the internet drives private profit by inviting people to 'play with it' (Dean 2010: 114). For Dean (2005: 53), 'governance by the people' has generally been thought of in terms of 'communicative freedoms of speech, assembly and the press, the norms of publicity, that emphasise transparency and accountability, and the deliberative practices of the public sphere'. Dean (2005: 53) argues that the 'communicative interactions of the public' have been replaced by the 'circulation of content and media chatter', which is 'supposed to impact official politics'. Dean (2005: 53) suggests that 'communicative capitalism designates the materialisation of democratic ideals in networked communication technologies'.

While it appears that audience interaction with the museum is democratising, a depoliticisation of audience expression takes place in the sense that viewing, creating and online connection is converted into user data. As the transformation to platforms that facilitate broad access, openness and participation becomes commonplace, meaningful political opportunity is eroded and the current arrangement of power is validated.

What does this mean? This perspective suggests that the mandate of museums to deliver access is shaped not only by how users engage with digital collections in participatory spaces but also by the affordances of the

82 *Negotiating museums as platforms*

Figure 5.2 This screenshot of Creative Commons example of *La Mona Lisa* by Jesus Belzunce is licensed under CC BY-NC-ND 2.0.

Source: https://creativecommons.org/licenses/by/2.0/?ref=ccsearch&atype=rich

media platform. This book has charted some of the approaches that a range of cultural institutions and their workers have adopted to maintain audience engagement. Everyone becomes a curator, friends become advocates of cultural content and the surveillance of audiences is normalised to enable personalisation and relationship management. Instead of it simply being something that digital platforms are 'doing' to the museum, the industry is steadily rearranging its 'production and distribution' to accommodate platform-based market structures (Nieborg and Poell 2018: 4287).

There is a belief that if the museum is to serve the public good and deliver social value, it should extend conversations to people using the formats and tools that are most relevant to the audience or audience type (demographic, psychographic, geographic). To do this, it has been important for the museum to adapt its physical and social spaces to embrace interactive participation. A prominent instance is the Los Angeles County Museum of Art (LACMA) in its second collaboration with the parent company of Snapchat, Snapchat Inc., which launched *Monumental Perspectives*, an AR exhibition that blended the efforts of Snapchat Lens Creators working with five artists to create virtual monuments that could only be viewed in specific places in the Los Angeles region (Vankin 2020). Because building new physical monuments is time-consuming and expensive, the virtual monuments were designed to reinvent the culture of remembrance and engage in conversation about long-suppressed histories and prove questions about the systemic perpetuation of inequality. Only viewable using the Snapchat app, users can employ their phones in specific locations in the Los Angeles region to view the virtual monuments. The institution describes the AR works on its website as an 'effort to reflect richer and more inclusive histories . . . by bringing untold stories of Los Angeles communities life' in order to 'explore current discussions around monuments and murals, representation, and American history' (LACMA 2020). As the exhibition rolls out, the museum intends to invite the community to view the new forms of monument and engage in ongoing discussion about current and historical identities. Interestingly, this exhibition is LACMA's (2019) second collaboration with Snapchat Inc., which is also on its Art + Technology Lab Advisory Board. In the first of such partnerships, visual artist Christian Marclay worked with Snapchat engineers to use algorithms to mine Snapchat ten-second videos to create five installations, two of which were interactive.

These two examples demonstrate an alignment between LACMA's curatorial function and the digital platform's automated editorial role. Snapchat is used to some extent to advance the political work of the institution. There is an increasing reliance on the media platform to not only enable the creation of cultural content but also to ensure that the artworks are seen. The AR virtual works become proprietary because they are only accessible using a privately owned platform. So, while the museum, artist and media provider endeavour to 'engage communities' in important conversations, a recalibration of the mode of access has taken place. Exhibits are potentially delivered through temporary ten-second geofilters, which are deleted unless they are added to the user's story. The promise of enhancing 'meaning creation' and the overall cultural experience of exhibitions can further drive museum workers, who have already begun hosting socially conscious exhibitions and outreach activities, to develop digital spaces to foster new forms of dialogue. Archivists, curators, directors, docents and historians are critical in applying enhanced digital platforms to push the museum to audiences using digital networks.

It is easy to forget that the enhanced access provided by digital platforms to culture comes with costs. We often fail to fully consider how power becomes concentrated in the hands of a few content providers. After all, the public forfeits control over how their data are collected and used in exchange for the benefit of new forms of cultural engagement and personalisation. Interactive participation repurposes the museum visitor as someone who provides data that will direct their material and cultural consumption. There is disparity between visitors participating in a setting where their data are collected for the purpose of enhancing the experience and when it is drawn on for marketing or unrelated purposes. Even the museum's own use of data collection, which endeavours to use devices to improve the visitor experience by matching visitors with calibrated content, alters the forms of looking and viewing that traditionally have taken place within these institutions.

It is clear that the museum aims to satisfy its users, rather than surprise and provoke them, with a potentially ever-diminishing echo chamber of cultural offerings. These practices realise a further segmenting and narrowing of the content to which the museum user is exposed and thwart wayfinding and traditional curatorial practices in favour of algorithmic personalisation. A foundation of teaching and learning is being exposed to new ideas or experiences (to broaden our minds). If the museum's agenda is to show us what we like without exposing us to what others like or dislike, is the museum fulfilling its own mission of pedagogy?

With the speed at which the AI, machine learning, big data, social networks and monitoring and surveillance technology are developing, the museum will always be a step behind the leading edge, while concurrently being a step ahead of the legislation around privacy and ownership of the data. At a critical time when museums are required to outsource overheads and costs wherever possible following shrinkages in visitor attendance and funding, Silicon Valley's megacorporations appear willing to fill this void. However, this externalisation of everything data driven is based on short-term gains driven by the market (or the pandemic) and the question would be whether the museum has adjusted or created a long-term strategy for its sustainability in light of this. From the perspective that access to collections is good for the audience, is there still value in an institution owning and displaying artefacts if the digital platform continues to provide open access to them with the option of facsimile in its common forms of AR, VR, 2D and 3D printing? As this book was moving into press, Google fired Dr Timnit Gebru, a prominent AI ethicist who was highly regarded for her work on algorithmic bias and face-recognition technology, after she criticised the company's attempts at diversity. The action prompted outrage from Google employees and a letter to Google's senior management requesting that the company apologise and reinstate her as co-lead of the company's ethical AI team (Singh 2020).

It is no longer enough to assume that museums don't have a stake in the decisions of media platforms. Instead, the museum must adopt leadership in ensuring that the governance structures enabling cultural access to collections operate in the public interest. While museum practitioners provided evidence that museums largely work to promote inclusive practices, it will become increasingly difficult to separate their initiatives from the platforms that help make them accessible. As they collaborate with technology companies that continue to bake themselves into the museum, ongoing engagement in conversations about the provision of trusted and reliable cultural content are crucial. AI facial recognition systems, for example, have been evidenced as unreliable, highlighting the requirement to integrate meaningful human intervention into the training of automated systems (Noble 2018).

Echoing global debates around the co-opting of news media content by digital platforms, the Australian government recently created innovative laws designed to force search and social platforms to pay for news material. The intent of the legislation was to reimburse commercial media organisations that have been decimated by advertising drift and to a lesser extent subscription losses (Zhou and Meade 2020). The scenario aligns with conversations around repurposing of museum content by digital platforms in recognising the cultural and public value of news and analysis that affords commercial value for the likes of Google and Facebook. These new media laws are messy but fundamentally encourage individual negotiations between media and platform entities. Already there has been pushback, with Google publishing an open letter to the Australian public highlighting that the legislation 'threatens to fundamentally damage Google Search' and instead proposes 'Google News Showcase' as a solution to paying for editorial expertise (Silva and Google 2020). Facebook, in contrast, has explained that Australian news content could be substituted for other content without any significant implications to its operating model, although this claim is disputed by legacy media producers (Meade 2020). This important proprietary tussle over public and cultural news content reflects similar tensions outlined here for museums. Crucially, it palpably demonstrates how it has become increasingly difficult to tempt the genie back into the bottle, given the ubiquity and dominion of platforms and to reclaim or reconfigure guardianship.

As the independently owned and operated model of museum platform configuration suggests, it is possible to work towards the creation of public spaces that leverage digital technologies yet are differentiated from prevailing models that use algorithmic reasoning and AI to direct consumption. It is essential that the museum strives to lead discussions about the need for inclusive, equitable and ethical applications of AI where it applies to user data from the platform. There is also a need to support the existing work of bodies such as Europeana and increase funding and investment for institutions to explore non-commercial platform alternatives. Exhibitions are crucial for engaging communities in ongoing discussions about the adoption of self-learning technology, transparency in the availability and repurposing of user data by marketers and in the proliferation of misinformation such as 'deepfakes' (the use of machine learning and AI to manipulate or digitally generate visuals, video and audio contents to be indiscernible from the original). That isn't to say that AI can't offer new insights into cultural collections. For example, San Francisco-based artist Nathan Shipley in 2018 created a Deep Fake of Salvador Dali for the Dali Museum in Florida that was capable of communicating with visitors and more recently used the technology to reimagine what historical figures in artworks such as the Mona Lisa might look like (Bored Panda and Hidrėlėy 2020) (see Figure 5.3). Instead, the museum must balance the tensions of machine learning and big data against the threats and ethical challenges of the governance of these systems. Safeguards for museums require a deliberate and sustained investment by governments, corporations and other organisations in artefact digitisation to minimise the occurrence of bias and other threats to collection access in terms of accountability, transparency, privacy and inclusiveness in order to adequately prepare the sector for new challenges.

By taking a production studies approach to the practices of museums and the outlook of its cultural workers, this book has defined the enactment of publicity in these institutions. One aim has been to highlight how fundamentally valuable media platforms have become to the delivery of cultural content and to raise attention to the museum adding another means of stimulating attention, affect and data collection. As the museum (and its workers) moves into the future, it must be cognisant that not everyone has consistent and easy access to communication technology, and the shift towards

Negotiating museums as platforms 87

Figure 5.3 *The Real Mona Lisa* by Nathan Shipley. This artist uses AI to re-create what important historical figures such as Mona Lisa might look like.

Source: Image of the Real Mona Lisa by Nathan Shipley.

designing technology-driven solutions will further highlight the digital divide. What the museum needs to truly remain an inclusive public sphere, both now and well into the future, is a decoupling of these institutions from commercial interests along with careful consideration of how media platforms that deliver access continue to be integrated into collections and the influence they are able to exert. Museums are essential to creating forms of social understanding and unity by promoting diverse perspectives, holding in trust for society objects that shape how we see the future.

Epilogue: COVID-19 and the museum

At the time this book went into production, the world in which we live had radically altered due to the outbreak of COVID-19 and its unprecedented spread globally. Immediately after the declaration of a pandemic, up to 90 per cent of the museums were forced to close. It is not surprising that this new landscape has dramatically altered how museums operate and has been pivotal in accelerating awareness by cultural institutions of the need to implement or expand their digital interfaces (ICOM 2020).

The ICOM produced a report in May 2020 that showed the digital activities of museums had increased over 15 per cent since COVID-19. The financial implications for these institutions have been significant. Even well-funded institutions such as the Metropolitan Museum of Art are predicted to lose up to $150 million from their budgets (Small 2020), with US museums forecast to lose as much as $33 million per day (Schulz 2020). For American institutions, at the very least, this has been exacerbated by the imposed increased dependence on private donors and benefactors, leaving these institutions highly vulnerable. Often reliant on a casual workforce, this has meant entire departments have closed. The MoMA in New York City has terminated the contracts of all its 85 freelance educators as a result of what the institution described as 'the unprecedented economic crisis caused by the COVID-19 pandemic and the Museum's closure' (Di Liscia 2020).

With the exception of China, which has been in the middle of a museum-building boom, there has been a neoliberal move towards decoupling museums from government. For private museums, fundraising, admission fees and revenue from restaurants and shops have all but dried up as a result of protracted closures. The impact has not been felt equally or been as dire for all museums. In the United Kingdom, for example, the National Lottery Heritage Fund has evinced greater sympathy for constraints in the sector, announcing grants of between £3000 and £50,000. Supporting this positive distribution of funds is a report by the Creative Industries Federation, a membership body that represents and supports the creative sector in the United Kingdom, which says that while the virus has been devastating, it estimates museums will lose only 9 per cent of their revenue (Bailey 2020). However, this prediction does not adequately capture the full and ongoing impact, which for many museums will involve permanent staff reductions, smaller operating budgets, fewer acquisitions and a diminished ability to present new exhibitions. Importantly, COVID-19 has drastically accelerated the adoption of digitisation, which has been taking place in museums for some time. It also places ongoing key debates raised here about access, engagement, publicity, digitisation, platformisation, funding and ownership into sharp relief.

Frances Morris, director of the Tate Modern, says that 'we're going to talk in terms of before and after. The virus will change a lot of things for art' (Dickson 2020). Other directors have raised concerns about losses from tourism along with soaring public debt, which will place increased pressure on already-stretched government funding (Cole 2020). In Australia, many regional institutions already impacted by diminished visitation as a result of the 2019–2020 bushfire season are experiencing further economic impacts as a result of long COVID-19 closures. For these regional institutions, funding resourcing and their long-term future are critical concerns. The UK Secretary of State for culture, media and sport, Oliver Dowden, recently advised British museum directors that they could adopt 'as commercially minded an approach as possible, pursuing every opportunity to maximize alternative sources of income' (Grosvenor 2020). The picture appears clear: the museum is entering an uncertain financial future, which is likely to mean less acquisitions, programming and educational activities at the very least. In the current environment, the policy imperative for museums to embrace digital formats has been further escalated by the pandemic.

Over the past three decades, the museum has been at a point when governance strategies have been shaped by failing market structures that propel the museum towards exploring alternate modes of delivery. We will observe museums continuing to demonstrate the social value of their institution in the context of an evolving ecosystem of scarce resources and funding cuts. Academic and arts and culture blogger Justin O'Connor (2020) equates the arts with welfare in discussing the 'protracted disinvestment in culture', stating that 'its leaders . . . have been forced to take handouts where they are reminded that their dependency on benefits would only be tolerated by taxpayers if they showed themselves to be deserving'.

In response to the pandemic, institutions have demonstrated their public orientation by actively seeking out new ways to support the communities in which they operate through the provision of digital community hubs and other online resources. There is a poignant desire to repurpose social media as sources of inspiration, connection and information, as spaces to download artworks, to exchange pictures and for forms of cultural expression and sociability. This continues a push towards museums experimenting with ways to make their collections available, moving towards a mode that is consistent with content that is distributed on media platforms. Museums are starting to discuss these issues among themselves largely because it has become increasingly necessary to explore sustainable revenue streams. Smartify (2020) recently launched an 'in app' museum shop, with the purpose of generating online shopping revenue to increase income in the sector.

The matter of exhibition fees and subscribers is of paramount interest, as visitors continue to log on to 'open access' collections remotely without paying to view content. The National Gallery in London recently trialled a half-hour video tour of its *Artemisia* exhibition as a way to generate income during COVID-19 closures (Marshall 2020). But set against the background of global technology companies, the museum's own attempts at incorporating technology can appear limited and must compete against other forms of content in already-saturated online spaces. In light of this, Netflix and other entertainment pathways become direct competitors for audience attention. A future option for funding may be to partner with the entertainment platforms, which have active subscribers and could offer culture package subscriptions to the existing audiences on these platforms. The onus will be on the institution to work with the platform to provide value content in order to remain within this network/channel and rely on it as part of their future. Indeed, the museum could and should continue to bring people together using digital means. And as visitors log onto virtual exhibits and engage with objects on social media using their smartphones during COVID-19 restrictions, they have grown accustomed to visiting museums from home. But without adequate public funding to support the adaptation to the digital era, it is likely that the provision of museum services will continue to be exposed to modifications that will erode its public role.

References

Aitken, Roger (2019). Can this man democratize and disrupt the art market? *Forbes*, 12 May. Retrieved from www.forbes.com/sites/rogeraitken/2019/05/13/can-this-man-democratize-disrupt-the-art-market/?sh=12a0b01d6303.

Bailey, Martin (2020). UK museum leaders distance themselves from controversial creative industries federation's report on coronavirus impact. *The Art Newspaper*, 9 July. Retrieved from www.theartnewspaper.com/news/museum-revenues-to-fall-by-just-9-seriously.

Bored Panda and Hidrėlėy (2020). 21 artificial intelligence recreations of famous paintings, historical figures, and cartoons by this artist. *Bored Panda*. Retrieved from www.boredpanda.com/author/hidreley-btu.

Budge, Kylie and Burness, Alli (2018). Museum objects and Instagram: Agency and communication in digital engagement. *Continuum*, 32(2): 137–50.

Carah, Nicholas (2014). Breaking into the bubble: Brand-building labour and 'getting in' to the culture industry. *Continuum*, 25(3): 427–38.

Cole, Alex (2020). What does the Covid-19 pandemic mean for Australian museums? *Museums Association*. Retrieved from www.museumsassociation.org/museums-journal/opinion/2020/07/10072020-what-does-the-future-hold-for-australian-museums/#.

Dean, Jodi (2005). Communicative capitalism: Circulation and the foreclosure of politics. *Cultural Politics*, 1(1): 51–74.

Dean, Jodi (2010). Affective networks. *Media Tropes eJournal*, 2(2): 19–44.

Dickson, Andrew (2020). Bye blockbusters: Can the art world adapt to Covid-19? *The Guardian*, 20 April. Retrieved from www.theguardian.com/artanddesign/2020/apr/20/art-world-coronavirus-pandemic-online-artists-galleries.

DiLiscia, Valentina (2020). MoMA terminates all museum educator contracts. *Hyperallergic*, 3 April. Retrieved from https://hyperallergic.com/551571/moma-educator-contracts.

Drotner, Kristen and Schrøder, Kim C. (eds) (2014). *Museum Communication and Social Media: The Connected Museum*. New York: Routledge.

Grosvenor, Bendor (2020). Be commercially minded or lose future funding: UK government's threat puts museums in peril. *The Art Newspaper*, 28 August. Retrieved from www.theartnewspaper.com/comment/dcms-leaked-letter-museums.

Henning, Michelle (2006). *Museums, Media and Cultural Theory*. New York: Open University Press.

Hitti, Natasha (2018). Christie's sells AI-created artwork painted using algorithm for $432,000. *De Zeen*, 29 October. Retrieved from www.dezeen.com/2018/10/29/christies-ai-artwork-obvious-portrait-edmond-de-belamy-design.

Hsi, Sherry (2003). A study of user experiences mediated by nomadic web content in a museum. *Journal of Computer Assisted Learning*, 19: 308–19.

International Council of Museums (ICOM) (2020). Survey: Museums, museum professionals and COVID-19. Retrieved from https://icom.museum/en/covid-19/surveys-and-data/survey-museums-and-museum-professionals.

Kidd, Jenny (2011). Enacting engagement online: Framing social media use for the museum. *IT & People*, 24: 64–77.

Lopes, Rui Oliveira (2020). Museum curation in the digital age. In Greg Hearn (ed), *The Future of Creative Work*. Cheltenham: Edward Elgar, pp. 123–39.

Los Angeles County Museum of Art (LACMA) (2019). *Christian Marclay: Sound Stories*. Los Angeles, CA: LACMA. Retrieved from www.lacma.org/art/exhibition/christian-marclay-sound-stories.

Los Angeles County Museum of Art (LACMA) (2020). LACMA × Snapchat: Monumental perspectives. Retrieved from www.lacma.org/art/exhibition/lacma-snapchat-monumental-perspectives.

Marshall, Alex (2020). Will art lovers open their wallets for online tours? *New York Times*, 9 December. Retrieved from www.nytimes.com/2020/12/09/arts/design/online-museum-tours-artemisia.html.

Meade, Amanda (2020). Australia is making Google and Facebook pay for news: What difference will the code make? *The Guardian*, 9 December. Retrieved from www.theguardian.com/media/2020/dec/09/australia-is-making-google-and-facebook-pay-for-news-what-difference-will-the-code-make.

Nieborg, David and Poell, Thomas (2018). The platformisation of cultural production: Theorizing the contingent cultural commodity. *New Media & Society*, 20(11): 4275–92.

Noble, Safiya (2018). *Algorithms of Oppression: How Search Engines Reinforce Racism*. New York: New York University Press.

O'Connor, Justin (2020). Art and culture after Covid-19. Moore institute. Retrieved from https://mooreinstitute.ie/2020/05/08/art-and-culture-after-covid-19.

Pesce, Danilo, Neirotti, Paolo and Paolucci, Emilio (2019). When culture meets digital platforms: Value creation and stakeholders' alignment in big data use. *Current Issues in Tourism*, 22(15): 1883–902.

Raphelson, Samantha (2017). 'I came, I saw, I selfied': How Instagram transformed the way we experience art. *NPR*. Retrieved from www.npr.org/2017/12/13/570558113/i-came-i-saw-i-selfied-how-instagram-transformed-the-way-we-experience-art.

Schulz, Abby (2020). Museums struggle as revenue plummets. *Penta*, 24 April. Retrieved from www.barrons.com/articles/museums-struggle-as-revenue-plummets-01587736656.

Silvia, Mel, and Google (2020). Open letter to Australians. Retrieved from https://about.google/intl/ALL_au/google-in-australia/aug-17-letter/.

Simon, Herbert A. (1971). Designing organizations for an information-rich world. In Martin Greenberger (ed), *Computers, Communication, and the Public Interest*. New York: Johns Hopkins Press, pp. 38–72.

Singh, Maanvi (2020). Google workers demand reinstatement and apology for fired Black AI ethics researcher. *The Guardian*, 17 December. Retrieved from www.theguardian.com/technology/2020/dec/16/google-timnit-gebru-fired-letter-reinstated-diversity.

Small, Zachary (2020). The Met announces dozens of layoffs as potential losses swell to $150 million. *New York Times*, 22 April. Retrieved from www.nytimes.com/2020/04/22/arts/design/met-layoffs-virus.html.

Smartify (2020). Exit through the virtual gift shop. Retrieved from https://about.smartify.org/blog/exit-through-the-virtual-gift-shop.

Vankin, Deborah (2020). LACMA turns to Snapchat again, this time for a virtual monuments project. *Los Angeles Times*, 8 December. Retrieved from www.latimes.com/entertainment-arts/story/2020-12-08/lacma-snapchat-virtual-monuments.

Vermeeren, Arnold and Calvi, Licia (2017). How to get small museums involved in digital innovation. In Luigina Ciolfi, Areti Damala, Eva Hornecker, Monika Lechner and Laura Maye (eds), *Cultural Heritage Communities: Technologies and Challenges*. London: Routledge, pp. 114–31.

Villaespesa, Elena and French, Ariana (2019). AI, visitor experience, and museum operations: A closer look at the possible. In *Humanizing the Digital: Unproceedings from the MCN 2018 Conference*, pp. 101–13. Retrieved from https://ad-hoc-museum-collective.github.io/humanizing-the-digital/chapters/13.

Zhou, Naaman and Meade, Amanda (2020). Facebook says it doesn't need news stories for its business and won't pay to share them in Australia. *The Guardian*, 15 June. Retrieved from www.theguardian.com/media/2020/jun/15/facebook-says-it-doesnt-need-news-stories-for-its-business-and-wont-pay-to-share-them-in-australia#:~:text=7%20months%20old-,Facebook%20says%20it%20doesn't%20need%20news%20stories%20for%20its,to%20share%20them%.

Index

3D 2, 4, 19, 29, 51, 85

access 2–3, 6, 8–11, 22–7, 33, 35, 39, 46, 50, 57, 59, 64, 81; to content 29–30, 32, 34–5, 40, 48, 67, 70–1, 80, 85–6; cultural 9, 14–16, 20–1; digital 8–10, 14, 34, 42, 66, 75, 78, 81; enhanced 40, 59; equal 21–3, 26, 64, 84; inclusive 24, 34–5, 58; open 13–14, 19–21, 25–31, 33–4, 39, 60, 85, 89; visual 19
accessibility technologies 21, 29–30
advertising 4, 60, 85
algorithms 2, 14, 35, 43, 46, 51–2, 59, 66–8, 70, 72, 83–6
Amazon 15, 47–8, 80
analogue museum *see* traditional
Andrejevic, Mark 9, 12, 38, 60, 70
Anne Frank House (Amsterdam) 57, 65
Application Programming Interfaces (APIs) 27–9
apps 2, 13–14, 28, 34, 41, 46, 51, *62*, 64, 66–70, 83, 89
archive *see* GLAM
art gallery *see* GLAM
artificial intelligence (AI) 2, 14, 29, 43, 51–2, 65, 71, 77–9, 84–6
Artvo (Melbourne, Gold Coast) 4, 7
Ask a Curator Day 64, 76
audience(s) 2 6, 45–7, 58, 63, 89; data 6, 52, 16, 76; excluded 22; multiple 20; online 31; opportunity 63; post/comment/rate 32, 39, 41, 47, *49*, 75–6; reach 34, 64; relationships 6, 59, 65, 68, 71, 83; senses 39; voice 12, 25

augmented reality (AR) 43, 46, 68, 70, 83, 85
Australian museums/galleries 11, 24–5, 30–1, 40; new media law 85
Australian Centre for the Moving Image (ACMI) 29, 43, 46, 53

Bennett, Tony 21–2
Berlin Declaration 27
blockchain museum 78
Budapest Open Access Initiative 27

cell/mobile phone *see* smartphone
Chan, Seb 29, 43, 46
chatbot 14, 57, 64–6, 72
Cleveland Museum of Art 29, 31
commodification *see* monetisation
communicative capitalism 81
Contemporary Art Museum (Wrocław) 52
Cooper Hewitt (New York) 29, 43, 64–5
copyright 27, 31, 33, 79
coronavirus *see* COVID-19
COVID-19 8–9, 12, 16, 43, 75, 85, 87–90
Creative Commons 26–7, 33–4, 80–2
cultural collections/content 2–3, 6, 45, 72, 83–6; control 31; creation 63, 71; curation 77; misuse 34, 65; publicly funded 26–9; sharing 27, 30, 70, 75
cultural institution *see* museum
cultural practices *see* museum
cultural practitioners/professionals *see* museum workers

curator/curation 6, 15, 59, 62, 75, 77–8
customisation *see* personalisation

data 3, 12–13, 14, 16, 28, 30, 51, 59; database/dataset 6, 11, 14, 43, 46, 51, 60; collection 9, 30, 38, 40, 45, 48, 51, 54, 60, 65, 84, 86
datafication 8, 10, 14, 40
dataveillance 14
Dean, Jodi 9, 12, 81
democratisation/democratic 1–2, 8, 12, 33–4, 43, 58–9, 66, 78, 81
digital collections-management systems 11
digital devices 1, 3, 14–16, 34, 40, 51, 53, 59, 60, 70, 78, 81; cameras 52, 67–8; Hi guide 43; 'O' pod 41, *42*, 43–5, 59; pen/stylus 43; screens 3, 50; sensors/y 20, 39, 50; *see also* smartphones
digital ecosystem(s) 3, 14, 16, 47, 66, 80
digital enclosure 60–1, 78
digital era 2–3, 72, 90
digital infrastructures 20, 30, 38, 43, 53, 63, 66, 80
digital innovation (of museums) 28, 30–1
digital layers 42, 44, 46–7, 51, 53, *62*
digital media sites *see* platforms
digital media technologies
digital technologies 1, 8, 11–13, 15, 19–20, 34, 40, 50, 52, *61*, 65, 72, 75, 85; literacy 77–8
digital transformations 20, 30, 44, 50, 60–1, 80
digitisation 3, 11, 15, 29, 32, 77–8, 80, 86, 88

education 1–2, 23–4, 48, 50, 53, 58
engagement 1–4, 13–14, 16, 23, 25, 28–32, 34–5, 42–3, 50–1, 54, 59, 60, 70, 75, 79–80, 88; with collections 39, 43, 45, 47–8, *61*, 63, 67, 81, 86; cultural 84; by museums 20, 62, 76, 83–4; participatory 52, 58; quality 65
Europeana 27, 78–9, 86
exhibit/ions 2–4, *5*, 7, 15, 57; on-site 46; pop-up 4; design of 43, 50

experience 32–3, 35, 48, 50, 59, 64–5, 72, 80; cultural 15, 22, 52, 63, 84; digitally enhanced 6, 46, 49, 60, *61–2*; immersive 19; mediated 11; multisensory 38–9; online/onsite 25, 38, 42, 44–5, 48, 50, 59; participatory 58; personalised 44; shared 44, *49*; social 39; user 3, 24–5, 29, 39–30

Facebook 14, 40, 51, 64–5, 85
facial recognition 29, 85
filters (art) 70, 76
Flickr 31–32, 34, 80
funding 2, 6, 8, 22–4, 26, 35, 84, 86, 88–90

Getty Museum 9
Gillespie, Tarleton 10
GitHub Repositories 28, 50
GLAM (gallery, library, archive, museum) 1, 26–7, 29–30; GLAM labs *see* labs
Google 24, 40, 85
Google Arts and Culture 13, 57, 67–8, *69*, 70, 80
GPS data 66, 71
guides 2, 39, 42–3, 51

Habermas, Jürgen 9–10, 12, 33, 58–9
handheld device(s) 41, 47–8
haptic gloves 19
hashtag 49, 63–4
heritage/heritage culture 1–2
Hirshhorn Museum (Washington) 43

IBM Watson AI app 52
ICOM (International Council of Museums) 2, 4, 24, 87
images *see* photographs
inclusion 2, 23, 81, 85
Indigenous collections 22, 31
Instagram 4, *5*, 6, 51, 63
intellectual property 27
interaction 6, 12, 31, 33–5, 38, 40, 44–6, 48–50, 63, 80–3; new forms of 6, 28, 50–2, 58, 62, 66, 75; interactive participation 2–3, 10, 12, 20, 43, 48, 58–9, 69, 83–4
internet 2, 20, 26–7, 30, 39, 47–9, 51, 60

Index 95

labour 4, 12, 43, 61, 70
labs 21, 29–30, 53, 64–5, 83
locative media *see* GPS
Los Angeles County Museum of Art (LACMA) 83
Louvre Museum (Paris) 57

machine learning 52, 59, 67, 84, 86
media platforms *see* platforms
media studies 6, 12
mediatisation 3, 8–9, 20, 57, 78
metadata 27, 29, 57
Metropolitan Museum of Art 8, 34, 87
Microsoft 29, 80
Mona Lisa 82, 86
monetisation 12, 14, 40, 71
monitoring 8, 12, 14, 16, 52, 61, 70, 83–4
multiple publics 20, 22, 24, 26, 34, 52, 58–60, 62, 66, 71, 75, 78; communicating with 64, 67
museum architecture/amenities 23–4, 39, 46, 52, 75; children's activity area 25–6; Braille text 23–4; free Wi-Fi 25, 50; labels 23–4, 39–41, 43–44, 54; lifts 24; maps 24, 43; parking 24–6; toilets 23–4; wheelchair ramps 23–4;
museum 1–4, 6, 12, 20, 33–4, 40, *61*, 67, 76, 80; accountability 3, 23, 25, 86; authority of 39, 59, 63, 66; blogs 12, 15, 29; characterising of 2, 3, 22, 24; civic/public purpose 1–3, 8, 20, 22–4, 28, 58, 64, 78, 83; education 58, 64, 80; ethics of 20, 24, 28, 51, 72; evolution of 21–2, 57–8; infrastructure 6, 20, 30, 35, 43, 53–4; mission 1, 10, 59, 65, 67, 71, 77, 84; non-traditional 4, 40, 54; online 6, 8–9, 11–14, 31, 79; on-site 6, 8, 12–15, 46; practices 1, 6, 11, 13, 20, 22, 43, 46, 48, 51, 53, 66, 78; public/private 1, 16, 21, 23, 53, 77, 88; research by 20, 23–4, 29, 54, 57, 71, 80; role of 6, 58, 90; smart 43, 49; workers 4, 11, 13, 15, 20, 24–5, 29, 31, 33–5, 38, 42, 45–9, 50–1, 53, 59, 61, 63, 66, 75, 77, 83–6; traditional 1–3, 6, 14, 30, 33, 54, 62, 75; physical 6, 31, 38, *61*; value of

8, 10, 13, 16, 23, 25, 28, 31, 35, 52, 57, 75, 78, 81, 83; websites 25, 29, 31, 64, 67;
Museum Next 12, 46, 52
Museum of Contemporary Art (Australia) *62*
Museum of Ice Cream (New York) 4
Museum of Modern Art (New York) 88
Museum of Old and New Art MONA (Hobart) 11, 38, 40–5, 59
museum practitioners/professionals *see* museum workers
museum studies 3, 6, 22, 77
museums as platforms 3, 78–9, 80–1
Museums Association 24

National Administration of Cultural Heritage (China) 9
National Gallery (London) 52–3, 89
National Gallery of Prague 19
navigation systems 42, 50, 53
near-field communictaiton (NFC) 43
neoliberalism 10, 88
Netflix 14–15, 48, 89
networks 3, 43, 63–4, 89
NeuroDigital Technologies (Spain) 19
new media/digital economy 1–3, 16, 52–3, 60
new museology 12, 22, 58
New Zealand Museum 25

online interfaces 20, 48, 50, 57, 65, 67, 78, 80, 87
online posting 6, *49*
openness principle *see* access, open

pandemic *see* COVID-19
participation 2, 4, 6, 8–9, 14–15, 22, 29, 32, 34–5, 39–40, 43, 45; discourse of 8, 12; logic 52; forms of 39, 70; platformised 62, 71; *see also* interactive participation
participatory culture 1, 46, 59, 66, 80; environment 10, 44, 81; technology 40, 59
partnerships 2–3, 19, 30, 34, 52–3, 65, 67, 71, 77–8, 83, 89
pedagogies/y, learning 39, 84
peer networks 4, 67, 69

96 Index

personalisation 2, 15–16, 35, 38, 48, 51, 53–4, 59, 60, 64–5, 71, 76, 83–4
photographs 9–10, 32, 39, 63, 67–8, 70, 76, 80; posting 2, 4, 61, 69; bans 6, 8; sharing 59, 64
Pinterest 34
platformisation/platformised 1, 4, 12, 20, 38, 53, 57, 62, 71, 77, 88
platforms 1–3, 6, 10–11, 14–16, 33–5, 40, 46, 48, 51–3, 59–60, 62–4, 67–8, 71, 75–6, 80–1, 83, 85–7; logic 40, 70, 52; norms 78; ownership 10, 84, 88
Portrait of an Articulated Skeleton on a Bentwood Chair 32
Portrait of Edmond de Belamy 78, *79*
Powerhouse Museum *32*
production studies methodology 11, 86
prosumers 12, 33, 75–6
public sphere 1, 3, 8–10, 16, 22, 57–9, 75, 81, 87
publicity 4, 6, 8–9, 12, 22, 52–3, 58–9, 81, 86, 88; critical 10, 33, 58; logic 16, 71; manipulative 10, 58; practices of visitors 9, 63; practices of museums 10, 13, 76; rational-critical 10, 58
publicness 9, 12, 71

QGoMA (Brisbane) 4, 11, *49*

RFID tags 41
Rijksmuseum 27, 31, 33–4, 78–9, 80

San Francisco Museum of Modern Art 28
Santa Barbara Statement 28
search engines 2, 6, 39
selfies 4, 6, 63, 70; stations *5*, 63, 76
sensing/sensory museum 15, 35, 38, 40–1, 43–5, 47, 50, 52–3
Sherratt, Tim 20
Shipley, Nathan 86–7
signage 39, 41, *49*, 62
Simon, Nina 8

smartphones 1, 7–10, 20, 38, 40–2, 47–8, 51–4, 60, *62*, 62–3, 66, 68, 83
Smithsonian 34
Snapchat 69, 83
social media 1, 3–4, *5*, 6, 45, 51, 53, 59–61, 65, 70–1, 84; engagement 9, 76–7, 89; logic 76; sharing 10, *49*, 60, 67–8; training 63, 77
sociality 4, 9
spaces 2, 30, 41–2, 52, 60, 65; digital/online 33, 75, 77, 84; inclusive 3, 14; museum 3, 13, 21–2, 29, 35, 41, 54, 61, 63; physical, 2, 33, 35, 60, 83; public 9, 13, 24, 35, 61, 86; social 76, 83
surveillance *see* monitoring

Tate Modern (UK) 50–2, 65–6, 71, 77, 88
technologies *see* digital
Te Papa (Wellington) 11
The Obliteration Room 4
TikTok 69
Touching Masterpieces 19
Turner, Graeme 12
Turrell, James *41*
Twitter/tweets 61, 64, 66

users *see* visitors

virtual museum 30
virtual reality (VR) 2, 19, 43, 85
visibility 4, 6, 9, 12, 14, 61, 63, 66
visitors 1–3, 6, 24–5, 38–9, 41, 45, 70; agency 47; attention 39, 44; behaviour 59; data 2, 81, 86; feedback 44, 47, 59; movement/navigation 35, 39, 40–1, 44–5, 47, 49; online 31, 33; on-site 1, 2, 48; satisfaction 46, 51; tracking 6, 15, 35, 45

Walsh, David 40, 42
wayfinding 39–40, 44, 48, 84
Wikimedia 32, 34
Wikipedia 77, 80